BELONGING TO THE PEOPLE OF GOD

BELONGING TO THE

Johanna sperl, illustrator

eople of God

by J. Bruce Weaver
Frank W. Klos, Editor

Lutheran Church Press
philadelphia

LCA SCHOOL OF RELIGION SERIES

A WORD OF WELCOME

FROM THE PRESIDENT
OF THE
LUTHERAN CHURCH IN AMERICA

*T*HERE is something symbolic in the fact that the hand outstretched on the first page of this book is mine. I welcome you not only with my own voice but also with the lips of all three and a quarter million of us in the Lutheran Church in America. We count ourselves rich in terms of the insights into the gospel which some of us have inherited and others of us have gained as adults. We are ready to share them eagerly with everyone who will listen.

This course is for inquiring minds. Let me accent the adjective first. Nobody is expected to commit himself in advance, of course, to anything he reads or is taught in the class. I for one would think it strange if you did so. That approach to life is not worthy of an intelligent adult. Altogether too many people carry with them too much uninspected religious baggage as it is. Never apologize for an alert look, for open ears, for a determination to look deeply and penetratingly into the things of faith. They are good.

We do not hedge about the noun either. Your mind is going to be addressed in this book. Godly sentiments, precious memories, a desire for fellowship are each a part of religion and, in proper balance, worthy elements of it. But let us be clear about it at once; no man is fully or safely Christ's until he has learned to love the Lord God with all his thoughts. That, frankly, is what we seek in ourselves as well as in you.

The first half of this book is concerned with a discussion of Christian faith and life. The balance of it is divided into sections on Luther's *Small Catechism*, worship, the Bible, church history, and the Lutheran Church in America. Each section will lay before you a great deal of basic information through the use of words and pictures, charts and diagrams. I hope you will feel that you have profited from our efforts.

Franklin Clark Fry

CONTENTS

CHRISTIAN FAITH AND LIFE

O Master, let me walk with thee
In lowly paths of service free;
Tell me thy secret; help me bear
The strain of toil, the fret of care.

Help me the slow of heart to move
By some clear, winning word of love;
Teach me the wayward feet to stay,
And guide them in the homeward way.

Teach me thy patience; still with thee
In closer, dearer company,
In work that keeps faith sweet and strong,
In trust that triumphs over wrong;

In hope that sends a shining ray
Far down the future's broadening way,
In peace that only thou canst give;
With thee, O Master, let me live.
                                    Amen.

The Nicene Creed

I believe in one God, the Father Almighty, Maker of heaven and earth, And of all things visible and invisible.

And in one Lord Jesus Christ, the only-begotten Son of God, Begotten of his Father before all worlds, God of God, Light of Light, Very God of very God, Begotten, not made, Being of one substance with the Father, By whom all things were made: Who for us men, and for our salvation, came down from heaven, And was incarnate by the Holy Ghost of the Virgin Mary, And was made man; And was crucified also for us under Pontius Pilate. He suffered and was buried; And the third day he rose again according to the Scriptures, And ascended into heaven, And sitteth on the right hand of the Father. And he shall come again with glory to judge both the quick and the dead: Whose kingdom shall have no end.

And I believe in the Holy Ghost, The Lord and Giver of Life, Who proceedeth from the Father and the Son, Who with the Father and the Son together is worshipped and glorified, Who spake by the Prophets. And I believe one Holy Christian and Apostolic Church. I acknowledge one Baptism for the remission of sins. And I look for the Resurrection of the dead, And the Life of the world to come.   *Amen.*

1

THE IMPORTANCE OF BELIEFS

BELIEFS are important. What you believe or do not believe
has a great deal to do with what you are and how you act. If
you believe that one political party offers a better program for
the country than others, the chances are that you are a member of that party. If you believe strongly in its program, you are
likely to be quite active on its behalf. Reflect awhile on your
habits, your loyalties, your activities, and examine the connec-
tions between your actions and the beliefs that underlie them.
Even though you may, on occasion, act contrary to some of
your beliefs, they are vitally important. Beliefs shape your
personality; they express the meaning and purpose you see in
your life, they give direction for action.

For effective, creative, and satisfying living, it is good to
probe your beliefs. Are they based on truth? Do they lead to
accepting the greatest values in life? Are they dependable in
times of confusion and crisis? The church offers you its witness to the beliefs that matter most—beliefs about God, about
the nature of man, about the purpose of life.

THE BASIS OF LUTHERAN BELIEFS

The Lutheran church uses two adjectives, "evangelical" and
"confessional," to characterize its beliefs. Both adjectives are
significant; both describe the climate in which the people of

God clarify their understandings, shape their attitudes, and prepare themselves for daily activities.

"Evangel" is a synonym for "gospel," the good news that God loves all people and seeks to help them through Jesus Christ. "Evangelical" is our way of saying that God's work on our behalf is the first and central concern in the life of our church.

"Confessional" means that we accept certain statements of faith, called the confessions, which proclaim what we believe and teach. These documents are collected in a volume called *The Book of Concord* and are part of our Lutheran heritage. As you become better acquainted with some of these statements, such as Luther's *Small Catechism* and the *Augsburg Confession*, you will discover that they are based solidly on the Holy Scriptures. For instance, the *Formula of Concord* says:

> . . . Holy Scripture remains the only judge, rule, and norm according to which . . . all doctrines should and must be understood and judged as good or evil, right or wrong.

Of this you can be sure: In the Lutheran church, both belief and practice are controlled by the gospel as it is proclaimed in the Scriptures. Understanding this principle of subjecting everything to the authority of the Scriptures is essential for understanding the beliefs of the Lutheran church.

From this point of view, then, there are no distinctive "Lutheran" doctrines; there are only biblically based teachings that present the truths of Christianity. In the pages that follow, our discussion of basic doctrine will always center on the teachings of the Scriptures.

As you study the church's beliefs, keep an open mind. Allow the witness of the Bible, of those people who lived close to God, to make its impact on your thinking. Evaluate the implications of these insights to your life. As you appropriate those beliefs that meet your deepest needs, you will feel drawn into the common faith and heritage of the people of God.

Lord, We Know You Love the World That You Created and Redeemed

We who stand in the world offer ourselves and our society for your blessing and healing.

We confess that we have failed to love as you did. We have been socially unjust, and our society is imperfect, fragmented, and sometimes sick to death.

Teach us your ways in the world and in this life which we share together. Don't let us restrict you to a narrow ghetto labeled "religion," but lead us to worship you in the fullness of life as the lord of politics, economics, and the arts

Give us light to seek true morality, not in narrow legalisms but in sacrifice and open responsibility. Show us how to express our love for you in very specific, human service to other men.

Lord, change our hearts from hearts of stone to hearts of flesh, and let us give thanks to you for all of life.

—MALCOLM BOYD

2

OUR DEEPEST NEEDS

HAVE you ever been lost? Let's say you are driving on a strange road at night and make a wrong turn at a crossroads. You are late for an important meeting and the needle on the gasoline gauge shows that the tank is close to empty. The darkness hides landmarks and so makes your road map useless; the combined prospects of missing your appointment and running out of gas lend a sense of urgency bordering on desperation. It is an awful feeling to be lost and caught in a predicament. A crisis like this helps us understand one biblical way of spelling out man's deepest needs. Man knows how easily he can lose his way, his sense of direction in life.

A SENSE OF LOSTNESS

The ancient writers of the Book of Genesis understood this human sense of lostness. They used stories of power and beauty to explain it. Read Genesis 2 as a description of the experience of every person in every age, and note what it says to you personally.

The Genesis stories make several sweeping affirmations: In a wondrous way God made man; God also gave man a meaningful role in the process of creation. In effect, he chose man to be a partner in the vital work of giving meaning and order to the world of living creatures. Seldom has the potential in man been given grander expression than in the biblical statement that he is created in the image of God. This does not mean a mirror likeness to God, but a capacity to reflect God's motivation of love in all human relationships. One of man's problems is that he seemingly cannot be content as the image of God. He wants to be his own man, not God's man. He wants to follow his own desires, make his own decisions, and run his world on his own terms. (This is the temptation to eat of the fruit from the tree of the knowledge of good and of evil which Genesis mentions.)

It is amazing how often we ignore the reminders that we are creatures rather than creator—pain and suffering, the necessity for toil, the inevitability of death, even the ominous hum of a hungry mosquito. We go on our way determined to do what we want with our lives—only to discover that, as we ignore God, we lose our sense of belonging and direction. We know the tragedy that results. We experience it personally; we see it in society as a whole. How different life would be if human talent, energy, intellect, and imagination could be used, in partnership with God, to continue the creative process of giving order and meaning to the world.

Just as "lost" is a good word to describe the human situation, the Bible suggests that man's deepest need is to be "found." Jesus told a number of parables to emphasize this: People become lost as a sheep is lost, by straying off on their own. They also become lost as a coin is lost, through the carelessness of others. Finally, they can become lost as a son is lost, through willful disregard of anything but his own desires. Read these Parables of the Lost in Luke 15. Notice, though, how Jesus stresses the fact that God seeks not to punish but to *find* the lost. This is the great and glorious truth of the gospel.

WHAT IS SIN?

Consistently, the Bible uses the term sin to describe man's lostness, his tendency to rebel against God. Paul understood this truth about human nature: "I can will what is right, but I cannot do it. For I do not do the good I want, but the evil I do not want is what I do" (Romans 7:18-19).

When people talk about sin, they usually refer to undesirable thoughts and actions, such as lying, cheating, stealing, adultery, murder. However, even though these misdeeds are destructive and dangerous, they are only symptoms of the real disease. Think how many times we commit acts which are against our better judgment and sometimes even against our will! How often we use the excuse "It just happened" as the only explanation for something we should not have done or said! But actually, nothing "just happens"; it is caused.

The church frequently calls man's inclination to turn against God "original sin." Sin has always been a part of mankind. This doesn't mean that we should blame Adam and Eve for our condition. The story of the fall of man in Genesis 3 really says that we sin not *because* Adam sinned but *as* Adam sinned. The concept of "original sin" acknowledges that sin is embedded in the human race, that it is a part of our personal nature.

Both the Bible and Christian tradition take sin seriously. They even personify it as an active malignant spirit in the world and call it Satan, or the Devil. This is one more way of emphasizing that our human situation is desperate. We are powerless to help ourselves no matter how hard we try. We need God.

Christianity begins to become a meaningful way of life only when we can honestly see ourselves as we are. Only then, when we acknowledge our creaturehood with all its failures and frailties, can the gospel reach us. At this point Christianity moves out of the realm of theoretical speculation and becomes a living experience.

In this discussion of the nature of man, our emphasis has been almost entirely upon the individual and his personal needs. But man does not live in a vacuum; he belongs to many communities. His nature therefore influences all areas of his social world.

STANDING TOGETHER

Why is it that even though most reasonable people agree that the best interests of all concerned are served by conditions of peace and brotherhood, we seem incapable of securing and maintaining these conditions? Does it make sense, with modern methods of transportation and communication, that even as we are growing closer and closer to each other physically, we foster conflicts that drive us further apart? Prejudice, crime, poverty, war—these proofs of man's inhumanity to man fill our contemporary world.

Another of the Bible's ancient stories, the Tower of Babel (Genesis 11:1-9), has something to say about this situation. This story points out a direct connection between man's defiance of God and his inability to communicate effectively with his fellowmen. You know the truth of this insight from your own experience. Whenever you have acted selfishly and begun to cater to your own whims, you have felt the effect of separation. This is an easy way to lose friends, alienate co-workers, and disrupt your family associations. When this happens, what good are explanations or rationalizations? Your actions speak louder than words. The principle works just as certainly when selfcenteredness is practiced by families, communities, nations, or even congregations. What is the answer to this problem? Our first impulse is to assume that working for individual morality will automatically create a moral society. But a good society can hardly be expected unless there are enough good people to make it possible.

Then, too, we hardly need to point out that no man, however upstanding he may be, is ever all good. Even those whom the church called saints recognized this truth about themselves. Since this is characteristic of all people, we have ample reason to doubt man's ability to build a good and perfect society by his own efforts.

Another important fact we cannot overlook concerns the nature of evil. Paul speaks about evil in terms of "principalities and powers." The New Testament records several incidents where Jesus healed people who were troubled by "demons." Such references to malevolent forces are ways of expressing the conviction that there is an active spirit of evil, call it what you will, affecting the individual and infecting all of his relationships. Even though we no longer use such terms for sin and evil, we can find ample evidence of their activity. It is for this reason that man, both as an individual and as a social being, stands in need of God.

The predicament of man and society is a persistent theme in literature, both classic and modern. You can explore the problem further from various points of view in such works as: John Milton, *Paradise Lost;* Herman Melville, *Moby Dick;* Albert Camus, *The Fall;* Fëdor Dostoevski, *Crime and Punishment;* T. S. Eliot, *The Wasteland;* John le Carré, *The Spy Who Came in from the Cold;* John Cheever, *The Wapshot Chronicle.*

THE CHURCH'S TEACHING

The main function of the Christian church is to proclaim the answer to man's needs by both doctrine and example. This proclamation begins by confessing faith in the living God. For centuries, Christians have used the words of the Apostles' Creed, "I believe in God the Father Almighty, Maker of heaven and earth." By this statement of faith, we affirm not only that God was the creator of life but that his relationship to his creation is a continuing one. In his *Small Catechism,* Luther gives a clear and simple explanation of this First Article of the Apostles' Creed:

> I believe that God has created me and all that exists. He has given me and still preserves my body and soul with all their powers. He provides me with food and clothing, home and family, daily work, and all I need from day to day. . . .

Notice how Luther emphasizes the fact that God is God, that we owe all we have and are to him.

But even as we repeat these solemn words of trust, the church knows that we will often forget or ignore our dependence on God, that we will therefore experience separation from God and alienation from our fellowmen, and that we will fail to realize the full potential of the humanity for which we were created. Therefore, the church reminds us that we stand under the mandate of God's law as well as his gospel.

LAW AND GOSPEL

In talking about the ways God comes to us and deals with us, we must remember that he makes certain requirements of us. As the God of all mankind, he describes what he expects of his people in their relationships with him and with each other. These requirements, these expectations, we call his law. Through deeply dedicated people like Moses, God made known his law to the world. God promises severe punishment for those who disobey his law. Actually, he doesn't need to punish us; we punish ourselves. When we go our own way, we turn love into hatred, trust into suspicion, respect for others into inhumanity, hope into despair.

Make no mistake about it. God's law is necessary. Men must realize that God demands social justice for all his people so that their rights as individuals may be preserved. But the law is not a set of arid prohibitions to prevent us from enjoying life. It is God's demand for justice for every man so that he may come to know the joy of life.

The law conveys in no uncertain terms God's judgment against sin. But it is also a dynamic and vital force which prods our consciences. When we measure ourselves against God's expectations of us, we sense our failure and the infinite gulf that exists between us and God. Luther described the law as a mask which God wears to remind us that we belong to him and that we have many responsibilities. God therefore gave the law to restrain sin, to make us realize our ignorance, our superstitions, and our flagrant disobedience of his will. This leads us to an awareness of our need for God's help.

The gospel proclaims God's offer of help in Jesus Christ to forgive us and to strengthen us for effective living as his people. This is the powerful insight Luther expresses in his explanation of the Second Article of the Apostles' Creed.

I believe that Jesus Christ . . . has redeemed me, a lost and condemned person, saved me at great cost from sin, death, and the power of the devil . . . with his holy and precious blood and his innocent suffering and death. . . .

REMINDER IN WORSHIP

As we worship each Sunday, using The Service as our guide, we begin with a confession of sin. The pastor then declares God's forgiveness. These twin themes are repeated in various forms throughout The Service, climaxed by the Agnus Dei (Lamb of God), which is sung just before the administration of the Lord's Supper. This emphasizes the fact that often when we are most aware of our separation from God, he is nearest to us.

The church acknowledges the constant need of all people for a savior. Through both its teachings and its worship, the church seeks to awaken in us a readiness to accept the gospel as the good news that God is concerned about us and that he offers us his richest blessings. In short, the church is an open channel through which God comes to us.

THE DIVINE INITIATIVE

Central to Christianity is the belief in a God who takes the initiative. He does not remain aloof from his world allowing his people to flounder in helplessness. He comes to our aid.

The God who comes to his people is one of the great themes of the Bible. The Bible sometimes may seem to be about the Jews, or the disciples, or the church. However, it is basically about God's creating, his calling people to be members of his family, establishing a covenant with them, giving them his law, delivering them from bondage, saving them through Christ, sending them as the church to witness to his world. This is the picture of God which Jesus reveals in those three memorable Parables of the Lost in Luke 15. God is not isolated "way up there" in heaven. He is active in his world, searching for his people, seeking to reconcile them with himself in the power of his forgiving love.

WHAT IS MAN?

Often, when we think of the vastness of our universe and the complexities of the modern world, we are apt to think of our lives as insignificant. Man is a statistic, a zip-code number, a digit on a television survey. Or is he? In the depth of his faith, an ancient psalmist found answers to his questions:

When I look at thy heavens, the work of thy fingers,
    the moon and the stars which thou hast established;
what is man that thou art mindful of him,
    and the son of man that thou dost care for him?
Yet thou hast made him little less than God,
    and dost crown him with glory and honor.
Thou hast given him dominion over the works of thy
        hands;
    thou hast put all things under his feet. . . .

—Psalm 8:3-6

Poetry often expresses the deepest truths with lively and imaginative figures of speech. The psalmist's confident perspective of man with all his potential is a healthy corrective to faulty thinking about man's worth. You are valuable—all people are valuable because of God. Yet though God wants us to say "yes" to his invitation to live as his people, he doesn't force us to do so against our will. God never infringes upon our basic integrity as persons; we can always say "no" to him. Integrity, in this sense, is but a part of a wider freedom with which we are endowed, and although there are obvious limits to that freedom, it is very real. But even to speak of integrity and freedom leads us to the purpose of living. What are we created for? The biblical answer is that we are created to be men, to live in trusting fellowship with God and with each other. This is the real meaning of being human.

In fulfilling our humanity, we realize our God-given purpose; in forgetting our humanity, we thwart God and frustrate our own destiny. When we ignore our place and function, we are challenging God's sovereignty over life. The challenge leads us to acts of rebellion and destruction to humanity. But even when it does, we still belong to God. Loving parents do not reject their children even when they are hateful and disobedient. They suffer with their children, seeking ways to help them become the kind of persons they could be.

The gospel is the good news that help has come. But has it? You can hardly escape wondering, as men in every age have done, just how the gospel is good news to you.

We are living in a rapidly changing world. Sometimes the changes are so swift and so radical that they leave behind all of our traditional ways of thinking. In our country, the process of urbanization has outstripped a way of life which, for many of us, had become almost synonymous with the Christian way of life. People who have grown accustomed to living under the threat of the hydrogen bomb are not overly terrified by thoughts of hell; those who enjoy affluence are not greatly intrigued by thoughts of heaven. Even the crises of living often seem to come in forms to which the gospel does not communicate. People who are schooled to rely upon scientific methods have difficulty in understanding or accepting the church and its faith. Modern problems such as automation, overpopulation, drug addiction, and space exploration have no specific biblical answers. Revolutions in moral standards have confused many people in their search for meaningful boundaries for their lives. Nevertheless, the nature and destiny of man does not change. He is the same whether he lived in a Palestinian clay-brick home long ago or lives in an apartment house today. Man always had and always will have the same basic human needs to be found, to be loved, to be guided toward self-fulfillment.

Lord God, heavenly Father, we know that we are dear children of thine and that thou art our beloved Father, not because we deserve it, nor ever could merit it, but because our dear Lord, thine only-begotten Son, Jesus Christ, wills to be our brother and of his own accord offers and makes this blessing known to us. Since we may consider ourselves his brothers and he regards us as such, thou wilt permit us to become and remain children of thine forever. Amen.

—MARTIN LUTHER

3

GOD IN CHRIST

PERHAPS you have had experiences which were so overpowering that your only reaction was to wonder at the mystery of it all. Paul felt that way about what God had done in Christ. After trying to explain to the new congregation of Christians at Rome how God helped men through Christ, he finally had to admit that it was beyond explanation. He could only exclaim joyfully:

> O the depth of the riches and wisdom and knowledge of God! How unsearchable are his judgments and how inscrutable his ways!
> "For who has known the mind of the Lord,
> or who has been his counselor?"
> "Or who has given a gift to him that he might be repaid?"
> For from him and through him and to him are all things.
> To him be glory forever. Amen.   *—Romans 11:33-36*

THE INCARNATION

Paul had to admit that the mighty act of God in Christ had no logical explanation. But even though we might not understand exactly how it happened, it was an action which a believer could accept and celebrate thankfully. In some wonderful way, God became man in order to meet us on our own level. We use the word incarnation to describe this momentous event.

"Incarnation" literally means "in the flesh." According to John's Gospel, "The Word became flesh and dwelt among us, full of grace and truth" (John 1:14). This is another way of saying that God came to this world in the human flesh of Jesus of Nazareth. There are several points that may illuminate the significance of this event. One is the hopes and expectations of the Jewish people before the coming of Christ.

THE COMING ONE

Back in the days of the great prophets such as Jeremiah and Isaiah, the Hebrews nourished a hope that God would again intervene in the history of his people as he had when he delivered them from bondage in Egypt (Exodus 1–14). Jeremiah expected this redeeming act of God to take the form of a new covenant which God would make with his people:

> Behold, the days are coming, says the LORD, when I will make a new covenant with the house of Israel and the house of Judah, not like the covenant which I made with their fathers when I took them by the hand to bring them out of the land of Egypt. . . . I will put my law within them, and I will write it upon their hearts; and I will be their God, and they shall be my people . . . for I will forgive their iniquity, and I will remember their sin no more.
> *—Jeremiah 31:31-34*

Isaiah, on the other hand, expected God to raise up another deliverer in somewhat the same pattern of Moses—but with significant differences. He describes the coming messenger of God, called the Messiah, as a man of suffering:

> Surely he has borne our griefs and carried our sorrows; yet we esteemed him stricken, smitten by God, and afflicted. But he was wounded for our transgressions, he was bruised for our iniquities; upon him was the chastisement that made us whole, and with his stripes we are healed. *—Isaiah 53:4-5*

Both Jeremiah and Isaiah sensed the implications involved in God's coming, but neither comprehended the full dimensions of the Incarnation. They did, however, provide a solid foundation for the messianic hope of the Jews which, through the long century and a half between the two Testaments, was altered by critical events. During this period, the Jewish dream of a restored kingdom dimmed under the conquests of the Near East by one conqueror after another, and the Jews transferred to the expected Messiah more and more of their frustrated longing for national independence and greatness. Also, and partially for the same reasons, the idea of the Messiah began to include the concept of resurrection and life after death for each believing person.

BOTH BODY AND SPIRIT

Another important aspect of thinking about the Incarnation is related to the biblical idea of man's nature.

Most of us tend to accept the Greek idea of man instead of the biblical doctrine of man, which is built on Hebrew concepts. The Greeks generally felt that man consists of two parts: a mortal body and an immortal soul. Hebrew thought, on the other hand, held that man is a unity, an integrated personality. Modern psychology supports this view. Body and spirit cannot be separated from one another nor can they be set over against each other. Man is always one and not two.

The doctrine of the incarnation, therefore, is based on the conviction that Jesus was both body and spirit, both God and man, a total personality. This insight Luther reflected in his explanation of the Second Article of the Apostles' Creed:

I believe that Jesus Christ—true God, Son of the Father from eternity, and true man, born of the Virgin Mary— is my Lord. . . .

Because we are accustomed to thinking that the physical nature of man is separated from his spiritual nature, we often have difficulty accepting on God's terms God's unique coming to us in Christ. We are baffled by the seemingly illogical com-

bination of body and spirit in one personality and easily fall
into the trap of wondering what percentage of Christ was
God and what percentage was man. The faith of the church
asserts that Jesus Christ was *completely* man and *completely*
God at the same time.

THE TITLES OF JESUS

Joseph and Mary, following the angel's direction, named the
baby Jesus, which means "God saves." Christ is the title he
bore to identify his mission to the world. The Greek term
Christ means "the anointed one" and corresponds to the Jewish concept of the Messiah. Properly, we should refer to him
as "Jesus the Christ" or "Jesus of Nazareth whom we believe
is the Christ."

Christ is not the only title applied to Jesus in the New
Testament. He is called Son of man, Son of God, light of the
world, eternal Son of the Father, Lord, and the Word. Each
of these terms helps explain the mystery of his being; each,
however, has its limitations because people differ in their understanding of what words mean. Take the title the Word, for
example. John 1:1 tried to use the Greek thought-forms of
his day to explain how the active God entered the world he
had created. He identified God's message of hope to men with
the living God himself.

THE COMING OF CHRIST

A number of events in your life stand out in your memory
as high points. Generally, these events so influenced you or
changed your life that you use them to recall other events that
came before or after. Your marriage, a birth, an award, a trip,
the death of a loved one—any number of life-changing events
have assumed special importance to you. Similarly, Christians
accept the coming of Christ as a momentous watershed event
for the world. It changed the course of human history.

You can't explain Jesus' influence on the world simply by
listing the details of his life. He was born into a humble family under hazardous conditions. He grew up in a carpentry

shop in one of the back corners of the civilized world. The details of half of his life, of his adolescence and early manhood, are lost in obscurity. His public ministry lasted only three years in a territory smaller than New England. Few recognized historians of his day did more than mention him; most ignored him completely. If it weren't for the New Testament, we would have little knowledge of his life. Even the Gospel writers who reported his life story had difficulty collecting biographical details to fill out their accounts.

Scholars generally agree that Jesus' teachings and sayings as recorded in the Scriptures are probably far from complete. Yet within a few years after his death, there were signs that Jesus of Nazareth was destined to have more than ordinary influence on the affairs of men. His disciples and other followers were fanning out in all directions to found congregations of people who acknowledged Jesus as their Lord. One of his most dedicated followers, Paul, described the powerful and growing influence of Christ in a letter to the mission congregation he had founded in the Greek city of Philippi:

> Have this mind among yourselves, which you have in Christ Jesus, who, though he was in the form of God, did not count equality with God a thing to be grasped, but emptied himself, taking the form of a servant, being born in the likeness of men. And being found in human form he humbled himself and became obedient unto death, even death on a cross. Therefore God has highly exalted him and bestowed on him the name which is above every name, that at the name of Jesus every knee should bow, in heaven and on earth and under the earth, and every tongue confess that Jesus Christ is Lord, to the glory of God the Father. —*Philippians 2:5-11*

Paul's letters to Philippi and other mission congregations, to individuals and groups who were beginning to exert their witness to the Christian faith in their community, comprise the bulk of the New Testament. When you combine and compare

Paul's witness with that of other New Testament writers, you can note those details in Christ's life which they believed to be of great importance: his birth, his baptism, his temptation, his ministry, his passion, his death and resurrection.

In addition to details of his life, the New Testament writers emphasized certain characteristics of Jesus. They stressed his divinity as well as his humanity. At times, however, it seems that the New Testament takes Christ's divinity for granted and reports incidents to underscore his humanity. There are references to his joy at a wedding celebration and his anger at the spectacle of the Temple being turned into a commercial enterprise. He is portrayed as a man who knew hunger, thirst, pain, and weariness, who wept at the death of a close friend, who wrestled with temptation, who made preparations for care of his mother even while he was dying.

The world has changed vastly in the twenty centuries since Christ. Our modern scientific minds are inclined to question his divinity rather than his humanity if we are disposed to be skeptical about him and his claims on our lives. It is much easier to accept Christ as a good man, a great man, the best man who ever lived, than it is to accept him as truly God in his manhood. Yet the New Testament consistently affirms that Christ is no less than both God and man.

In one sense, the event which the New Testament writers describe is complete, final. This is true when you consider the event in terms of what God did for men in Christ. Paul says, "God was in Christ reconciling the world to himself, not counting their trespasses against them. . . ." Looking at it that way, all that needs to be done has been done: God's act of redeeming love is complete, final, and trustworthy. However, Paul goes on to say, ". . . And entrusting to us the message of reconciliation. So we are ambassadors for Christ, God making his appeal through us. We beseech you on behalf of Christ, be reconciled to God" (2 Corinthians 5:19-20). This brings Christ out of ancient history into our own world, into our own personal experiences.

THE NEW COVENANT

Another helpful way to explore the significance of the Incarnation is to think about the idea of the covenant.

The word covenant implies an agreement between two parties based on mutual trust and affection. The Old Testament reports several occasions when God established a covenant with his people as the foundation for a continuing, close relationship with them. In his covenant with Abraham, God pledged greatness for his people and the giving of a son to Abraham to be the beginning of the people, a host of descendants to outnumber the stars. Abraham, his family, and his followers pledged to live in faithfulness to the God who chose them as his own.

The covenant God established with Moses in the desert wilderness was far more elaborate, incorporating a series of laws including the Ten Commandments. God pledged to his people that even as he had brought them out of captivity in Israel, he would continue to be their God. The people, for their part, were to keep God's laws. But, more importantly, they were to remember all that God has done for them despite their unworthiness. The law was not intended to fence in God's graciousness, but to serve as a way through which it would be expressed in every human relationship and in all the activities of life. The great prophets directed their efforts toward alerting the Jewish people to the power of the covenant and challenging them to develop appropriate responses of obedience and mission.

With this background, the Incarnation was seen by many as a new covenant, and therefore the collection of writings that witnessed to this mystery bore the title the "New Covenant" or, its more familiar translation, the "New Testament."

UNIVERSAL AND TIMELESS

The writer of the Epistle to the Hebrews speaks of Christ as "the same yesterday and today and for ever," to voice the Christian conviction that what God has done in Christ applies to all creation and for all time. This universality is echoed in John's familiar words:

> For God so loved the world that he gave his only Son, that whoever believes in him should not perish but have eternal life.   —*John 3:16*

THE ATONEMENT

One of the best-known words used to describe the universal and timeless work of God through Jesus Christ for the benefit of all people is the term atonement.

Can you remember when, as a child, you willfully disobeyed your parents? The disobedience, whatever it was, made you feel guilty. You wanted to avoid your parents; you were afraid of the consequences. Finally, either your parents discovered the transgression or you confessed. Even if you were punished, you can remember the relief you felt at being freed from guilt, the joy of renewing your trusting relationship with your parents. The cause of your fear and dread was removed by either their action or yours. The result was a healed and restored relationship, a reconciliation. Atonement means just that, a reconciliation between God and man, a restoring of God's relationship with man, a healing of the bonds of trust and love broken by man's sin.

In the Old Testament, the idea of atonement was linked with sacrifice. In the Jewish sacrificial rite, the penitent person usually offered an animal to God to symbolize the surrendering of his own life. The blood of the animal on the altar was supposed to symbolize the blood of the sinful person who deserved to die because he had turned against God. The Hebrews believed that the sacrifice system was established by God himself to provide a means of bringing about forgiveness and deliverance. However, some of the prophets, like Isaiah, sensed that God was greater than the image men had of a petty tyrant who demanded a payment of blood—any blood—to make up for wrongs. In his great love for his people, God also suffered for them when they cut themselves off from him. Read Isaiah 53, the portrait of the Messiah as the suffering servant who bore the sins of others, who was wounded for the transgressions of others and bruised for their iniquities, who healed others by his suffering. Isaiah's poetic insights were made facts in the ministry of Jesus. He fulfilled Isaiah's concept of a God who cares so much about his people that he is willing to suffer himself throughout his own life and work. The church therefore has used the rich imagery of Isaiah to interpret Christ's act of atonement on the cross as part of God's divine plan.

Each time we repeat the Nicene Creed, we confess our belief in the atonement Jesus Christ has accomplished through his own perfect life:

And [I believe] in one Lord Jesus Christ, the only-begotten Son of God, Begotten of his Father before all worlds, God of God, Light of Light, Very God of very God, Begotten, not made, Being of one substance with the Father, By whom all things were made: Who for us men, and for our salvation, came down from heaven, And was incarnate by the Holy Ghost of the Virgin Mary, And was made man; And was crucified for us under Pontius Pilate. He suffered and was buried; And the third day he rose again according to the Scriptures, And ascended into heaven, And sitteth on the right hand of the Father. And he shall come again with glory to judge both the quick and the dead: Whose kingdom shall have no end.

THE KINGDOM OF GOD

Throughout the atonement, God creates a new form of life for his people so they can live with him and with each other in an atmosphere of mutual love and trust. The New Testament uses a number of terms for this new form of life: living under the new covenant, living a newness of life, being born again, and being in Christ. Jesus embodied all of these ideas in his references to the kingdom of God.

From the beginning of his earthly ministry, Jesus confronted men with a challenge to live in God's kingdom:

"The time is fulfilled, and the kingdom of God is at hand; repent, and believe in the gospel."   —*Mark 1:15*

Jesus clearly believed that it was his mission to inaugurate the kingdom of God. This was in full accord with the Hebrew prophets, who had looked forward to the day when God would assert his sovereignty over all creation in a visible and indisputable way.

Most of the Jews were displeased at Jesus' teachings about the kingdom. They had grown accustomed, during their checkered history, to think of God's kingdom politically. They believed that one day God would intervene, punish their enemies, and establish a holy nation where they and their descendants could live in peace. The Messiah was to be their champion, a new David mighty in battle who would lead them to this great victory. Not only did Jesus fail to measure up to the image of a warlord, but he taught that God's kingdom was more of an inner reality than it was an actual geographical entity.

Matthew collected a number of parables which Jesus told about the kingdom to help his followers understand the phenomenon of God's rule over the lives of men. Read Matthew 13 carefully to see how each parable helps shape a meaningful concept of the kingdom.

Jesus taught that the kingdom is not a realm in the ordinary, physical sense of the word. It cannot be measured in square miles nor can it be located precisely on a map. The kingdom exists in the lives of people committed to God, and through them the kingdom spreads to others. The emphasis is on changed people rather than on a changed society.

Further, Jesus taught that the kingdom is in the process of coming. Although Jesus generally defined the kingdom as the action of God in the midst of his people in the present, he still taught his disciples to pray "Thy kingdom come." This prayer is a reminder that while we live in God's kingdom now on the basis of our faith, we look forward to the time when all of mankind can share in God's rule.

In a certain sense we can think of Jesus as the personification of the kingdom. We often think of the President of the United States or the Prime Minister of Canada as personifications of the vital life of the nations they serve: They speak for their country, represent it in international relations, and sometimes even suffer and die for it. As we are confronted by Jesus to accept his lordship in our lives, we are simultaneously invited to live with him in his kingdom now and through the life to come.

Jesus pointed out that the kingdom represents a new opportunity for people to see value and purpose in their lives. At the same time it places upon them the responsibility to serve in their communities as "the salt of the earth," as the "light of the world." Most of us have yet to explore fully this revolutionary aspect of the gospel's claim on our loyalties.

To accept God's forgiveness through Christ, to live in his kingdom, Jesus says that we must "repent and believe in the gospel." This is the wholehearted response God expects of us. Repentance means, of course, sorrow for sin, but primarily it means willingness to change allegiance and direction. For most of us this change is radical, for it means that we must substitute God's will for our own will and God's way for our way. Repentance can be painful, but the pain is soon forgotten in the joy of accepting God's gifts. Only by repenting can we believe in the gospel, which means simply putting our obedient trust in God above everyone and everything that the world has to offer. Remember, it is God's act in bringing in the kingdom that calls for our thankful response of repentance and faith. We do not earn his gifts; we couldn't, even if we worked hard at achieving holiness for a lifetime. We can only accept his gifts on his terms and, under his guidance, move from spiritual adolescence to new levels of spiritual maturity and responsible partnership with him.

JUDGMENT AND GRACE

There is a paradox in the concept of the atonement: How can God be a God of justice and a God of mercy at the same time? If God is just, then man's sin deserves not only condemnation but punishment; if God is merciful, then he will forgive the sin. Can God be both at the same time? Doesn't God's merciful act in Christ seem to destroy his justice? Doesn't letting man off the hook so easily make it irrelevant whether or not man sins?

An ancient story may help us to resolve the paradox of God's grace containing justice and mercy simultaneously:

A king once waged a long but fruitless struggle against the poison of corruption in his kingdom. Finally he issued a stern decree that anybody who was caught taking bribes, no matter who he was, would be punished with forty lashes. The first to be discovered taking bribes was his own mother, whom he loved and honored as a faithful son. When the king heard this dreadful news, he secluded himself for three days to consider how he could possibly treat his mother with both justice and love. After the third day he ordered the people and all the great in his kingdom, including his mother, to be summoned to the court of judgment. There the king pronounced the sentence: The king's mother is condemned to receive forty lashes, but the punishment is to be executed—upon her son, the king! The king put off his crown and his royal robes, allowed himself to be bound to a stake, and suffered his mother's punishment.*

Sin that needs forgiveness cannot be erased simply like wrong answers on a chalkboard. If it could, we would either seriously doubt God's justice or discount the seriousness of sin. The cross, however, makes it clear that sin always costs pain and suffering. Like the king in the story, God in Christ

---

* Quoted in Eberhard Müller, *Conversation on Faith* (Philadelphia: Muhlenberg Press, 1961), pp. 118-119.

took upon himself the punishment his sinful people deserved. Nowhere has the world seen justice and mercy linked together more dramatically than in the spectacle of the dying Christ saying, "Father, forgive them; for they know not what they do."

THE WORD OF GOD

Perhaps you have known people who have such a reputation for honesty and square dealing that you can say of them, "Their word is their bond!" This is the equivalent of saying that when these persons promise to do something it is as good as done. Similarly, when we refer to God's message to man as his Word and use the term "the Word of God," we should think of God's activity in fulfilling his promises. What God speaks is not only as good as done, it is done. The Word of God, therefore, leads to the atonement because God promises us that he will be our God and do everything possible to help us live as his people. Joseph Sittler explains the link between the Word of God and the atonement this way:

> The biblical term for the fact *that* God reveals and *what* God reveals is *the Word.* . . . Every manifestation of himself in creation, mercy, judgment, salvation, is a Word of God. This means that the Word of God is first of all what God says to us, the content of his communication. But God wills to do more than *say something to us,* more even than to *communicate* something to us. The content of his communication is *himself!* . . . All verbal forms, all means of communication through speech, prove too weak . . . ; only what we call the Incarnation, the coming of God to us in Jesus Christ, is sufficient. Here we see what is said and the *one who says* in conjunction; he who speaks is himself present, and his speaking is not merely speech but life, the life of a person.*

* Joseph Sittler, Jr., *The Doctrine of the Word* (Philadelphia: Board of Publication of the United Lutheran Church in America, 1948), p. 62.

To call Christ the incarnate Word of God is to remind ourselves that God was working both in and through him on our behalf. The Word of God really comes to us in many ways: through the living presence of Christ in our hearts, through the pages of the Bible, through the sacraments and preaching, through the life of the church and the witness of dedicated Christians. The proclamation of the Word, in whatever form, always conveys to the believer the atoning work of Christ.

THE CHURCH AND THE ATONEMENT

Martin Luther once said that the church without the Word would be nothing. That is true because the church exists as the fellowship of the people of God to be an important channel through which God's Word comes to every generation. The announcement of the kingdom of reconciliation and forgiveness is the center of the message of the church, the core of its fellowship, and in a very real sense the source of its mission to the world. Each time we worship using The Service, the pastor speaks the reassuring words of the Declaration of Grace:

Almighty God, our heavenly Father, hath had mercy upon us, and hath given his only Son to die for us, and for his sake forgiveth us all our sins. To them that believe on his Name, he giveth power to become the sons of God, and bestoweth upon them his Holy Spirit. He that believeth, and is baptized, shall be saved. Grant this, O Lord, unto us all.

JOHN 15:1-16

"I am the real vine, and my Father is the gardener. Every barren branch of mine he cuts away; and every fruiting branch he cleans, to make it more fruitful still. You have already been cleansed by the word that I spoke to you. Dwell in me, as I in you. No branch can bear fruit by itself, but only if it remains united with the vine; no more can you bear fruit, unless you remain united with me.

"I am the vine, and you the branches. He who dwells in me, as I dwell in him, bears much fruit; for apart from me you can do nothing. He who does not dwell in me is thrown away like a withered branch. The withered branches are heaped together, thrown on the fire, and burnt.

"If you dwell in me, and my words dwell in you, ask what you will, and you shall have it. This is my Father's glory, that you may bear fruit in plenty and so be my disciples. As the Father has loved me, so I have loved you. Dwell in my love. If you heed my commands, you will dwell in my love, as I have heeded my Father's commands and dwell in his love.

"I have spoken thus to you, so that my joy may be in you, and your joy complete. This is my commandment: love one another, as I have loved you. There is no greater love than this, that a man should lay down his life for his friends. You are my friends, if you do what I command you. I call you servants no longer; a servant does not know what his master is about. I have called you friends, because I have disclosed to you everything that I heard from my Father. You did not choose me: I chose you."

THE NEW ENGLISH BIBLE

O Lord, make me the instrument of thy peace.
Where there is hatred, let me sow love;
   Where there is injury, pardon;
   Where there is discord, union;
   Where there is doubt, faith;
   Where there is despair, hope;
   Where there is darkness, light;
   Where there is sadness, joy;
O Lord, grant that we seek
   not to be consoled, but to console;
   not to be understood, but to understand;
   not to be loved, but to love.
   For it is in giving that we receive,
   in forgetting that we find ourselves,
   in pardoning that we are pardoned,
   and in dying that we are born to eternal life. Amen.
                        —FRANCIS OF ASSISI

4

The NATURE OF FAITH

MANY people who have obvious physical handicaps prefer to be treated as though their handicaps do not exist. They do not want to be babied; they want to be independent. But if you have ever tried to ignore the handicap of a friend, you know how difficult it is to treat him as if he were perfectly normal. You have to restrain yourself to keep from offering a helping hand to a blind person making his way across a room, or assisting someone on crutches to get into a car even though you know they want to make their own way. If you can understand a relationship with such people that respects their desire for independence and, at the same time, lets them feel that they can call for help if they need it, then you have a good insight into the nature of faith. God encourages us to keep a sense of independence even though we have to live with handicaps caused by sin and, at the same time, he is willing to come to our aid when we need him. The Lutheran confessions have much to say about our faith relationship with God and frequently use a theological phrase, "justification by grace through faith," to describe the process. Let's look at the profound concepts in the phrase: justification, grace, and faith.

JUSTIFICATION

The term justification has its origin in the language and practice of the law courts. The purpose of the court is to guarantee that justice is provided for every person. If a person who is tried for wrongdoing can be proved to have had a sufficiently just and legal reason for his actions, he is acquitted and freed from custody. As far as the court is concerned, he is to be treated as though he had never been accused at all; he is justified.

The religious use of the term justification is related to our understanding of man as a willful breaker of God's laws who must stand before God for judgment. In a sense, he is on trial for his life. He is helpless; he can do nothing to help himself. He must throw himself on the mercy of God his judge.

One of the Lutheran confessional documents, the *Formula of Concord,* gives classic expression to the way God in his love justifies the lawbreaker:

> The righteousness which by grace is reckoned to faith or to the believers is the obedience, the passion, and the resurrection of Christ when he satisfied the law for us and paid for our sin. . . . This righteousness is offered to us by the Holy Spirit through the Gospel and in the sacraments, and is applied, appropriated, and accepted by faith, so that thus believers have reconcilation with God, forgiveness of sins, the grace of God, adoption, and the inheritance of eternal life. —*Solid Declaration, Article III*

Several decades before the *Formula of Concord* was written, one of Luther's friends, Philip Melanchthon, had explained justification as one of the basic theological principles of the Protestant Reformation. In the *Augsburg Confession,* Melanchthon was quite specific:

> . . . Men cannot be justified before God by their own strength, merits, or works but are freely justified for Christ's sake through faith when they believe that they are received into favor and that their sins are forgiven on account of Christ, who by his death made satisfaction for our sins. This faith God imputes for righteousness in his sight. —*Article IV*

The doctrine of justification is very important because it deals with the question of what it means to be a Christian. You can talk and think at length about ideas such as the atonement and the kingdom of God and still not get deeply involved in a meaningful relationship with God. These teachings present God's mighty act of redemption in a factual, objective way. Justification, however, has a deep personal meaning; it links God's forgiving love with our individual need for help. To be justified means that you are given a status which you would not otherwise have and which you cannot by any means at all attain for yourself. God accepts you as righteous by allowing you to share the righteousness of Christ. This God does wholly and always out of his grace.

BY GRACE

Let's explore this word grace. Imagine that you are deeply in debt. Time and again you have gone over your resources and prospects, and there is just no way out. Then a friend of yours bails you out by making enough money available to restore your credit and give you a new start. You would never cease to be grateful to the friend, particularly if he were someone who was in no way obligated to help you and did so entirely out of generosity.

Read carefully what the writer of the Letter to the Ephesians says about grace:

But God, who is rich in mercy, out of the great love with which he loved us, even when we were dead through our trespasses, made us alive together with Christ (by grace you have been saved), and raised us up with him, and made us sit with him in the heavenly places in Christ Jesus, that in the coming ages he might show the immeasurable riches of his grace in kindness toward us in Christ Jesus. For by grace you have been saved through faith; and this is not your own doing, it is the gift of God—not because of works, lest any man should boast.

—Ephesians 2:4-9

Now reread Jesus' Parable of the Prodigal Son (Luke 15: 11-32). The role of the father in the parable is a beautiful description of God's gracious attitude toward us. In passing, it is worth noting that the attitude of the older brother is quite characteristic of many of us. God's willingness to receive those who have sinned against him seems almost too good to believe; it is especially hard to believe when it is applied to someone else. It is helpful to think of grace as God's prevailing attitude toward you in somewhat the same sense that a normal parent has a prevailing attitude of concerned love toward his child. The child may disobey, may turn against the parent, may even run away from home and hurt the parent in many other ways; yet the parent's motivation to love his child is a strong force. This love tends to remain constant and dependable even when parental displeasure and anger are openly displayed. Psychologists say that the growing child needs assurance of his parent's unchanging love toward him. The unchanging, trustworthy, loving attitude of God toward men makes it possible for Christians to have a similar assurance, knowing not only that they are saved by grace but that with God's help they can live by grace as well.

Paul chose his words carefully to make sure that new Christians understood this:

> Since we are justified by faith, we have peace with God through our Lord Jesus Christ. Through him we have obtained access to this grace in which we stand, and we rejoice in our hope of sharing the glory of God. More than that, we rejoice in our sufferings, knowing that suffering produces endurance, and endurance produces character, and character produces hope, and hope does not disappoint us, because God's love has been poured into our hearts through the Holy Spirit which has been given to us.   —Romans 5:1-5

This assurance has vital sustaining power for guiding us through all the events and conditions of life, especially in those critical times when our inadequacy is most apparent—times of sickness, hardship, bereavement, and death. Christianity offers no guarantee that we will escape difficult experiences; it does offer assurance and strength to face these experiences triumphantly. He who accepts God as his heavenly Father can say with Paul:

> For I am sure that neither death, nor life, nor angels, nor principalities, nor things present, nor things to come, nor powers, nor height, nor depth, nor anything else in all creation, will be able to separate us from the love of God in Christ Jesus our Lord.   —*Romans* 8:38-39

The New Testament consistently proclaims that the redeeming love of God is as eternal as God himself. In Christ, his constant attitude of love and mercy is revealed to us in a dramatic way. In Christ, we are able to see and feel that God has indeed invaded our realm of life and has assumed the burden of our sinful flesh. In Christ, God is meeting us where we are. He has come into human life to meet us at the point of our greatest need. God always takes the initiative to find us and win us back to him. But we need to accept his grace, his freely given justification. His gifts, as great as they are, are not irresistible. God forces no man against his will to be united with him in bonds of love. Clearly then, God's offer of forgiveness and help demands that we make a decision whether we will or will not link ourselves to him. Choosing him, accepting his grace, and allowing his will to guide our wills are all involved in the positive response we call faith.

THROUGH FAITH

Faith is a key word in the Christian's vocabulary. But we are so accustomed to using the word loosely that we need to stop and think about what it really means. There is a careful distinction made between grace and faith: It is *by* grace and *through* faith that salvation comes. God reaches down his hand to us and we reach out to clasp it. This is the rich symbolism behind the colophon of the Lutheran Church in America's Parish Education Curriculum. Take another look at the artist's impression of this colophon on page 19. Faith is simply receiving gladly all that God's grace provides.

No book can explain fully the miracle of faith. It goes far beyond words. You have to experience faith to understand its power. You can read a book on how to drive a car or you can listen to a friend's experiences of driving a car, but you do not know what it really means to drive until you get behind the wheel yourself. You may believe completely what you are told and the knowledge thus acquired may be accurate and trustworthy, but it is never quite the same as the insights gained through experience. Every vital experience of life involves the whole person, his intellect, his emotions, his senses, his actions. Faith is no exception.

Christian faith grows stronger as your experience the grace of God in your life. The message of the gospel, the love and support of fellow Christians, encourage the growth but are no substitutes for your personal faith. As time goes on, you will learn deeper doctrinal truths about the nature of Christianity, but your faith is not dependent on your intellectual assent to all the church's teachings. Your faith is your acceptance of God and your willingness to trust him.

Christian faith is something like that of a child on a wall who jumps off into the waiting arms of his father. He knows that he will be there to catch him. Faith in God is like that child's trust—complete, unswerving, and strong. Perhaps that is why Jesus told us that our faith should be childlike: ". . . Whoever does not receive the kingdom of God like a child shall not enter it" (Mark 10:15).

The gospel as the Word of God has the power to create and nurture faith. In one sense, hearing the gospel or reading the Scriptures is the experience out of which saving faith can grow. God works through his Word to bring a person to the place where he recognizes his sinful condition, asks for help, and trusts in God to bring it. Hearing the gospel, however, does not create faith automatically; there are always some who have heard the gospel and rejected personal involvement with God. But without hearing and believing the gospel we could not experience faith in God at all.

THE DIMENSIONS OF FAITH

The unknown writer of the Letter to the Hebrews offers an excellent description of faith. (See Hebrews 11—12:2.) He begins by defining faith as "the assurance of things hoped for, the conviction of things not seen," and concludes by pointing out the source of faith, "looking to Jesus the pioneer and perfecter of our faith. . . ." In between these guide points he calls the roll call of great Old Testament heroes of faith. Take time to read these brief biographies of people who experienced faith and grew in their relationship with God. Notice how each person cited wagered his life on God by accepting God's direction for his life. His goals, the things "hoped for," the things "not seen," were accomplished as he walked in obedient trust with God.

Faith implies complete trust. Martin Luther once said that our greatest sin is our unwillingness to trust God's forgiveness. This trust enables us to relax in the midst of the terrors and dangers which threaten our lives, for we learn that God strengthens us and cares for us when we need his help. Your faith comes to your aid in facing these dark moments because you believe that God will always help you deal with life's problems creatively and triumphantly.

The whole concept of faith is exciting. J. S. Whale calls attention to faith's radical and joyous dimensions:

> In short, faith means trusting Jesus: just that, in its heartbreaking simplicity. And justification means that we sinners are put right with God, here and now, by that faith alone. If this is true, it is the most amazing truth under heaven. The Gospel declares that it is true. It is paradoxical, irrational and non-moral, that God should love

THE NATURE OF FAITH 47

the sinner and justify the ungodly. It is beyond reason and it makes nonsense of the wisdom of this world (I Cor. 2:6 f.). The elder brother was entirely right, on his strictly moralistic premises, in regarding it as unfair: it transcends every legal way of thinking, every system of moral book-keeping, every calculus of rewards and penalties; it refuses to put divine grace on a tariff. It is the Lord's doing and it is marvelous.*

FREEDOM IN CHRIST

Sometimes people think Christianity is a joyless, prune-faced, folded-hands sort of life that is opposed to all human pleasures. Unfortunately, Christianity has become for many a religion based on restrictions and prohibitions. Nothing could be further from the truth. Being Christian does not depend on what you don't do but on what you do. Faith gives you a new freedom to enjoy life widely and richly. Paul speaks frequently of sin as bondage and describes faith as the key that unlocks its fetters to free the slave. Apart from the religious truth of this, psychologists agree that those who have guilt complexes will continue to suffer mental anguish until they are liberated from the worries that weigh them down. Centuries ago, Christ told us the best therapy for guilt was faith in God. Through our trusting acceptance of God's forgiveness, guilt is destroyed and we know the exhilaration of freedom.

Every person knows that one day he will die. However, the dread of death can be a paralyzing form of bondage. Our faith in God gives us the assurance that we will pass through death into another form of life with our Lord. Already through Christ's resurrection from the dead, God has proclaimed what is in store for those who trust him.

Even if God in Christ had done nothing more than make provision for releasing us from the weight of guilt and removing our dread of death, the gospel message would be the best

* John S. Whale, *The Protestant Tradition* (London: Cambridge University Press, 1955), pp. 70-71.

news any man ever heard. To the degree that we have faith, this liberating power operates in our lives; we are freed from bondage to sin and death. This is the cornerstone of Christianity.

LIVING BY FAITH

Most people are surprisingly conservative. Some like novelty for its own sake but the vast majority of people feel uncomfortable in the presence of anything radically new. This was true in Jesus' day as well as our own. Many of the conservative Jews who called themselves Pharisees were scandalized and frequently angered by Jesus' seemingly preposterous claims that he had come to fulfill the law. They felt that he had overstepped the boundaries of decency and good order when he implied that the whole body of sacred law could be fulfilled in a new and revolutionary way. No Pharisee could fulfill all the laws and since, in their opinion, the Pharisees were God's best people, they felt it was blasphemy for some upstart to claim that he knew the way it could be done. For this reason few Pharisees followed Christ.

What Jesus had done was to negate the traditional values and customs of the Pharisees and others like them. He proclaimed a new way of life built on guidance for living rather than obedience to laws. This new life involved much more than avoiding wrong actions. The new life, the free life in Christ, called for disciplined words and thoughts as well. Look at some illustrations Jesus used in the Sermon on the Mount to stress his point. For example:

> "You have heard that it was said to the men of old, You shall not kill; and whoever kills shall be liable to judgment. But I say to you that every one who is angry with his brother shall be liable to judgment. . . . You have heard that it was said, You shall not commit adultery. But I say to you that every one who looks at a woman lustfully has already committed adultery with her in his heart. . . ." —*Matthew 5:21-22, 27-28*

Jesus' interpretation of the law as applying not only to our deeds but our thoughts and attitudes makes us realize even more the impossibility of achieving perfection. We know how much we need God's strength and forgiveness in the freedom he has given us through our faith.

Jesus' explanation of what it really means to live with God also brought opposition, because it undermined a Jewish point of view. The Jews had made the law a sort of guardian for the gates of heaven. It was a series of obligations man had to meet to prove his worthiness of God. This emphasis on the law had reached such a point that it distorted religion: It looked backward and bound man to the past. In effect, it turned the honorable traditions of the Jews into a burden that hampered effective and joyful life in the present and cast a heavy shadow upon the future. This is what Jesus changed through his ministry. He showed how men could live the kind of lives God expected of them by living with God first of all. Those who were willing to live the new life in faith were freed from the law's demands because they voluntarily disciplined themselves to let God's love shine through their thoughts, words, and actions.

Even today, people have trouble comprehending what it means to live by the gospel. It is easier to live by the law, and much more comfortable. You know generally what you should do and what you should not do in many areas of human conduct. However, there are twin temptations that complicate living by God's law alone. One is the tendency of some to multiply the number of petty sublaws until life seems little more than a straitjacket. The other is the tendency to feel superior because they have followed the law's demands. The difference between living according to the law and living in the light of the gospel can be illustrated by the difference between painting by filling in numbered spaces and painting creatively. Painting by numbers may be fun for awhile, but it isn't satisfying in the long run. The person brushing the specified colors into numbered shapes soon realizes that he is really a prisoner

This love of which I speak is slow to lose patience—it looks for a way of being constructive. It is not possessive: it is neither anxious to impress nor does it cherish inflated ideas of its own importance.

Love has good manners and does not pursue selfish advantage. It is not touchy. It does not keep account of evil or gloat over the wickedness of other people. On the contrary, it is glad with all good men when truth prevails.

Love knows no limit to its endurance, no end to its trust, no fading of its hope; it can outlast anything. It is, in fact, the one thing that still stands when all else has fallen.

For if there are prophecies they will be fulfilled and done with, if there are "tongues" the need for them will disappear, if there is knowledge it will be swallowed up in truth. For our knowledge is always incomplete and our prophecy is always incomplete, and when the complete comes, that is the end of the incomplete.

When I was a little child I talked and felt and thought like a little child. Now that I am a man my childish speech and feeling and thought have no further significance for me.

At present we are men looking at puzzling reflections in a mirror. The time will come when we shall see reality whole and face to face! At present all I know is a little fraction of the truth, but the time will come when I shall know it as fully as God now knows me!

In this life we have three great lasting qualities—faith, hope and love. But the greatest of them is love.

—J. B. PHILLIPS

of those who designed the project. On the other hand, if this same person uses his paints on a blank canvas to create whatever he feels, he experiences a kind of happiness. He has used his talents to fashion something all his. Living by the gospel is God's invitation to each person to contribute himself to life, to meet each new situation and each person as a free son of God and serve them according to their needs, imaginatively and creatively. This does not mean that we no longer need God's laws, for we still fall far short of committing ourselves totally to him. Through his laws, he shows us our failures and helps us sense our constant need of his help in Christ.

BOTH SAINTS AND SINNERS

To say that a Christian is both saint and sinner at the same time may sound like double-talk, but it is true. It is a way of expressing a profound truth about the nature of man and his relationship with God.

How would you react if someone called you a saint? If your notion of a saint is an other-worldly person with an extra measure of piety and angelic behavior, you might be flattered—but, knowing yourself, you would have trouble accepting the tribute. But as a Christian, you ought to accept it. A saint is not a sort of super-holy person; it is anyone who has accepted God's gift of forgiveness in Christ. The term saint is synonymous with believer. It means that you are accepted by God as righteous because of Christ. A saint is someone who belongs to the people of God. Notice how the Apostles' Creed insists on calling the church the communion of saints. You are a saint, not because you are perfect or godly or pious, but because you are given that status by God.

If you are at all honest with yourself, you know that you are still a sinner even though you accept God's gift of special status. That basic rebellious frame of mind still exists and therefore you need the prodding of the law to remind you of every separation from God and of your constant need for his forgiveness. Christianity is not an escape from the world of reality. On the contrary, it enables people to live in that world creatively, accepting themselves as they are and, through God's help, becoming more the kind of persons God planned them to be. It is in this tension of seeing ourselves as both sinners and saints that we come to understand something of what it means to be justified by God's grace through our faith in him.

> *Lord, be Thou within me, to strengthen me; without me, to keep me; above me, to protect me; beneath me, to uphold me; before me, to direct me; behind me, to keep me from straying; round about me, to defend me. Blessed be Thou, our Father, for ever and ever. Amen.*
> —Lancelot Andrewes (1555-1626)

5

The church and its purpose

As members of the people of God, Christians hold the church in high regard. This is their opportunity to join with fellow Christians in worship and service; this is their communion of saints in which they are confronted by God's Word and through which they mobilize their resources to witness to their faith. In his explanation of the Third Article of the Creed, Luther says:

> . . . In this Christian church day after day he fully forgives my sins and the sins of all believers. On the last day he will raise me and all the dead and give me and all believers in Christ eternal life.

WHAT IS THE CHURCH?

Unfortunately, many of us use the term church in a bewildering variety of ways. Everyday references and theological definitions are sometimes poles apart.

The most common reference to church in ordinary conversation is also the narrowest definition. People speak of "my church" or of "going to church." When they do so, they are actually referring to a specially designed building, located at a specific address, which houses a congregation and provides a base for the congregation's activities. But the building is merely a convenience and is quite incidental to our concept of church. Buildings are static and valueless by themselves. It is the purpose for which they are used that determines their importance.

A broader use of the word church links it with the local congregation rather than a particular building. The congregation is, according to both the dictionary and the biblical usage, "an assembly of persons met for worship and religious instruction." But this, too, is an inadequate definition of the church, for it does not take into account the more or less continuous sense of belonging together with fellow Christians in other congregations. Perhaps the congregation is best thought of as the local expression of the worldwide church fellowship.

There is still another way to define the church—as a denomination or a confessional body. When we refer to the church as "the Lutheran church," we are thinking of the worldwide family of Christians who subscribe to the Lutheran confessions. But the qualifying adjective "Lutheran" still limits the definition to our particular family of Christians. For practical purposes we usually add geographic distinctions as in the "Lutheran Church in America" and narrow the concept even further.

Let us define the church in its broadest sense as simply the people of God. It is this concept of the church that we want to consider. The relationships of the congregation, the denomination, and the worldwide church are carefully explained in the Constitution of the Lutheran Church in America:

> The Church exists both as an inclusive fellowship and as local congregations gathered for worship and Christian service. Congregations find their fulfillment in the universal community of the Church, and the universal Church exists in and through congregations. This church [the LCA], therefore, derives its character and powers both from the sanction and representation of its congregations and from its inherent nature as an expression of the

broader fellowship of the faithful. In length, it acknowledges itself to be in the historic continuity of the communion of saints; in breadth, it expresses the fellowship
of believers and congregations in this our day.

—LCA Constitution, Article IV, Section 2

When we refer to the church as a congregation or a denomination or as "the church," we are speaking of but one church
which we experience in different ways. When you become a
church member, you belong to "the church" within the particular witness of a denomination, and you choose a local congregation as the primary place for your worship and service.

THE NATURE OF THE CHURCH

Both the Apostles' and Nicene Creeds have something to
say about the nature of the church. The original version of the
Apostles' Creed says simply:

I believe in The Holy catholic Church, the Communion
of Saints. . . .

The Nicene Creed expands this somewhat:

And I believe one Holy catholic and Apostolic Church.

Putting these two statements together gives a significant picture of the nature of the church. As Christians, we believe in
its importance as the communion of saints. We also believe
that the church has certain vital characteristics. It is one, holy,
catholic, and apostolic. Let's examine these ideas carefully.

THE COMMUNION OF SAINTS

As justified sinners, we are bound together into a communion or community. That is, we hold something in common
which also holds us in a unique relationship to each other.
This cohesive force is the experience of the love of God in
Christ. Therefore, we can and do say that the church is of
divine origin, not only in respect to its starting point in history,

but wherever and whenever men have accepted God's grace. Even though the church takes institutional forms, similar to other social forms of fellowship and community, it is quite different. Christians believe that the church is held together by God's love. Its fellowship includes communion with God, as well as fellowship with fellow Christians, unbound by ordinary limitations of space and time. And its is through this fellowship that the Word of God comes to the world.

THE CHURCH AND THE WORD OF GOD

God's living, hopeful message to the world comes clearly through the church fellowship. The living Word of God is, therefore, the core of the Lutheran doctrine of the church.

The church is the assembly of saints in which the Gospel is taught purely and the sacraments are administered rightly.   —*Augsburg Confession, Article VII*

Historically, Lutherans have used this statement to identify the nature of the church and to test both doctrines and practices in the light of the gospel. The statement reminds us that the basic reason for the church's existence is the Word of God, which comes to us through the Scriptures and through Christ the living Word as well as through the sacraments.

When the Word of God meets life, something happens: Life is brought under God's judgment and mercy, faith is born, and community is created. In short, the church comes into being. Indeed, it is continuously coming. It is an event which is always occurring. When we speak of "the church," we ought to try to think of it in this way rather than confining it to any of its institutional forms. Ezekiel, the Old Testament prophet, offers a fine parable of the church (47:1-12). He describes a river issuing from the threshold of the Temple, flowing out into the countryside. As it flows, it gives life and nourishment to everything it touches and, instead of being diminished in volume, the farther it flows the wider and deeper it becomes. That is "the church" as God intends it to be.

THE CHURCH IS ONE

The first among the distinguishing characteristics of the church is its oneness. This is hard to accept in the face of so many competing denominations in almost every community. If the church is one, why must there be Methodists, Baptists, Presbyterians, Episcopalians, several brands of Lutherans, Roman Catholics, the Eastern Orthodox, and many other groups all of whom claim to be channels for God's truth? The divisions of Christianity are not only a source of confusion but sometimes cause people to refuse to choose a denomination.

No one can deny that disunity is often a hindrance to cooperative efforts. But there is another side to the picture. Those who criticize the church most severely for its divisions usually assume that there was a time in the days of the apostles, or perhaps in the Middle Ages, when the church was perfectly united in body and spirit. This simply was not the case, a fact which becomes apparent as you read the Book of Acts and Paul's Epistles. There has always been diversity in the church and no doubt there always will be. People are not alike in their tastes for music and art, or even in the ways in which they like to work. Similarly, all people do not worship God in the same way. But all denominations can lead their people to sense their special place in the worldwide church. Diversity itself is not bad. It becomes harmful only when it erupts into sinful competition, jealousy, and hatred.

UNITY IN DIVERSITY

Paul wrestled with the problem of unity in one of his letters to the mission congregation at Corinth. He developed a vivid metaphor that helps us to see that unity is possible even in the midst of diversity. Let's look at several of his points:

> Now there are varieties of gifts, but the same Spirit; and there are varieties of service, but the same Lord; and there are varieties of working, but it is the same God who inspires them all in every one.   —1 Corinthians 12:4-6

For just as the body is one and has many members, and all the members of the body, though many, are one body, so it is with Christ. For by one Spirit we were all baptized into one body—Jews or Greeks, slaves or free—and all were made to drink of one Spirit.

For the body does not consist of one member but of many.   —*1 Corinthians 12:12-14*

Now you are the body of Christ and individually members of it.   —*1 Corinthians 12:27*

In Colossians 1:18 and 2:19, Paul adds that Christ is the "head of the body." The church, with all of its different members and all of its different denominations, is his body. Loyalty to Christ is the real unity of the church.

The figure of a body with each of its different parts performing a separate function for the whole and yet with each dependent upon all the others, all forming an organic unity related to and controlled by the head, is a good working principle of what the church is or, more accurately, of what the church ought to be.

Your own relationship with the people of God will be greatly enriched if you think of it in terms of belonging to the "body of Christ." To a very real degree, the health of the whole body of Christ is dependent on your healthy participation in a congregational family. Whoever you are, you have a positive contribution to make to Christ's work through your active partnership in your congregation's ministry.

So when we speak of the unity of the church, we are talking about a unity that exists in spite of a rich and creative diversity. It is a unity given to those who confess Christ as their Lord. By this confession of faith, they are led to find peace in God through Christ. God has extended this same grace, accomplished the same reconciliation, and nurtured the same hope in all believers, incorporating them into a fellowship which is the body of Christ. Though witness to this unity is often obscured by sin and weakness, the church is still one.

THE CHURCH IS HOLY

Holiness is another characteristic of the church. Most people tend to think of holiness as the equivalent of goodness and therefore consider a holy person someone who has an unblemished character and is morally pure and ethically superior. People who match this description are hard to find, if indeed you can find any at all. However, this is not what holiness really means. Holiness is a religious concept that is actually divorced from legalistic right and wrong. Holiness describes man's standing before God. No man can restore his relationship with God by his own efforts. But God accepts the righteousness, or holiness, of Christ in place of that which we cannot attain. God gives us our holiness in the same way he gives us our sense of unity—by his own free will. It is not accidental that the words "holy" and "whole" come from the same root. To be holy is to be complete. Holiness is an attribute of God who is whole or complete, and through the church, the body of Christ, we participate in his holiness.

THE CHURCH IS CATHOLIC

The third characteristic of the church is its catholicity. The term catholic means universal. All Christians are members of the one, holy, catholic church (as the original text of the creed says). The word catholic conveys two significant thoughts. Wherever the church exists, it offers all the gifts of God through Christ. The second implication is that, in its fidelity to the gospel the church witnesses to the truth that God's grace is for all men without distinction or exception. The church belongs to all Christians regardless of sex, race, class, clan, or nation. This suggests that the church wherever it is, in whatever form, must proclaim the gospel. It also means that all artificial barriers must come down. There must be no exclusion from the church on the basis of social standing, economic level, educational attainment, or any other artificial distinctions. The church supports the integrity and the dignity of every human being. God loves all men. Christ died for all men. God invites all men to become his people. Without a sense of catholicity, the church is less than it should be.

THE CHURCH IS APOSTOLIC

The term apostolic is the last in the series of characteristics by which the creeds describe the church. The belief that the church is apostolic refers first of all to the conviction that the church's teachings are in basic agreement with the teachings of the apostles. The apostles were men of their times who quite naturally couched the gospel in the meaningful thought-forms of their age. Nevertheless, the central Christian message is enshrined in their writings.

Suppose you were writing an account of the great event such as the Lewis and Clark expedition to explore the territories added to the United States through the Louisiana Purchase. You would probably put more trust in the information Meriwether Lewis and William Clark supplied in their journals than in information gained from books written two hundred years later. You might have to worry over the explorers' frequent misspellings and their out-of-date figures of speech, but you would know you were sharing the experiences of men who were there. Similarly, we rely on the witness of the apostles because they give us the only firsthand information we have of the life and work of Christ. They saw his miracles happen; they heard his words or listened to those who did hear them. It makes sense for the church to remain as true as it can to the apostolic understanding of the meaning and effect of Christ's ministry.

There is another highly significant meaning of the word apostolic which we should not overlook. Literally, the word apostle means "one who is sent." So when you confess that you believe the church to be apostolic, you are accepting your part in the church's responsibility to go into the world as God's special group of messengers. The church is not only a repository for truths of the past, it is also sent on a mission to make those truths relevant to the present.

THE PURPOSE OF THE CHURCH

Suppose you were asked to decide what features of your congregation rightfully deserve recognition. Would you want your congregation to have its reputation based primarily upon the excellence of its worship with masterful choirs, a good organ, and enthusiastic congregational participation? That wouldn't be a bad thing, would it? In fact, it is the sort of excellence toward which any congregation could strive without shame. How about good preaching and dependable pastoral care? Those are excellent indications of congregational vitality. Or a thorough program of Christian education that provides imaginative, attractive, and effective education for people of all ages? Surely, no congregation could feel itself complete without the best program of religious education it could possibly develop. These features, plus a high quality of congregational fellowship and good physical facilities, are certainly what most people look for when they are choosing a congregational home. Each of these features is important, even necessary, to the functioning of a healthy, well-rounded congregation. But do you notice one thing? Everything we have mentioned is really geared to serving the members of the congregation, to "taking care of our own."

But what part do these features play in the really basic purpose of the church? This purpose was expressed by Jesus in one of the last directions he gave his disciples:

> "Go therefore and make disciples of all nations, baptizing them in the name of the Father and of the Son and of the Holy Spirit, teaching them to observe all that I have commanded you. . . ." —*Matthew 28:19-20*

If the church thinks of itself as the body of Christ, or as the people of God, it is quite clear that its mission is outward, not inward. First of all it is designed to serve the world, and then its own needs.

The congregation's activities, such as worship, study, and fellowship, are all important, but they are not ends in themselves any more than the total life of the church is an end in itself. The church is at its best when it is most deeply aware of its role as a messenger of God. It makes a profound difference in the quality of your support of your congregation and your participation in its ministry when you feel that you belong to a group recruited to serve others rather than a social club that can bestow benefits on you. The real benefits of belonging to God's people come into our lives when we seek first to help the church fulfill its mission of proclaiming, witnessing, and serving.

STRENGTH IN WEAKNESS

Perfect realization of the church's mission is admittedly unattainable. Human imperfection and failure prevent it. As an institution, any congregation is subject to the same temptations that afflict its members individually, and succumbs with the same dismaying ease and frequency. Thus, there is always a tension between what the church is in the mind and purpose of God and what the institution exhibits in its life and work. However, it is a creative tension that God uses to keep the church on its toes, stretching and growing.

Your attitude toward the church and its purpose therefore is vital to your own personal growth as a modern disciple. In the *Large Catechism,* Luther describes the believer's relationship with the church:

> I believe that there is on earth a little holy flock or community of pure saints under one head, Christ. It is called together by the Holy Spirit in one faith, mind, and understanding. It possesses a variety of gifts, yet is united in love without sect or schism. Of this community I also am a part and member, a participant and co-partner in all the blessings it possesses. I was brought to it by the Holy Spirit and incorporated into it through the fact that I have heard and still hear God's Word, which is the first step in entering it. . . . Until the last day the Holy Spirit

remains with the holy community or Christian people. Through it he gathers us, using it to teach and preach the Word. By it he creates and increases sanctification, causing it daily to grow and become strong in the faith and in the fruits of the Spirit.　　　　　　　*—Second Part: The Creed*

THE MEANS OF GRACE

The electric power that lights our cities and turns the wheels of industry is furnished by great hydroelectric dams and generating stations around the country. The dams and generators could go on producing electric current forever; but without reliable means of transmission, industries, stores, and houses would not benefit. So it is with the boundless power of God's grace. Within the church, there are certain ways through which this is transmitted to people. These are called the means of grace.

Scripture teaches us that the grace of God is "transmitted" to the believer by the Word and the sacraments. Because of the broad meaning of the term Word of God, it is hard to distinguish between Word and sacraments without artificially putting them in two completely different categories of meaning. Actually, the sacraments are the Word of God in a particular and personal form.

THE SACRAMENTS

The sacraments are not primarily lessons or ceremonies; they are acts that do something. In and through them, the crucified and risen Christ comes to us personally. The sacraments are the Word of God at work among us: imparting forgiveness of sins, newness of life, and eternal hope; strengthening the faith in which we receive and trust these gifts; and uniting us in fellowship with God and with each other. We simply accept these gifts of God. The effectiveness of the sacraments depends on nothing else. Neither the faith nor the character of the person who administers the sacraments to us has any influence on their validity.

Sometimes people are skeptical that the grace of God could possibly be communicated by such commonplace earthly elements as water or bread and wine. But it is precisely this factor of ordinariness that gives the sacraments their special usefulness. Basically, we define the sacraments as certain acts which use earthly elements, which are performed on Christ's command, and which bring God's promise graphically into our lives. The sacraments connect the supernatural with the natural, divinity with mortality, heaven with earth. In essence, the sacraments tell us that God is here working for us.

At this point Baptism and the Lord's Supper become distinctive. There are no other acts of the church in which the fullness of the work of Christ is conveyed to the believer and made his own in such a vividly personal way.

BAPTISM

Sometimes Baptism is considered simply as an initiation rite to admit people to the privileges and responsibilities of church membership, or a special christening ceremony by which a baby is given his name publicly and his presence as a member of a human family is officially acknowledged. But Baptism is much more. Paul noted its great significance for the Christian throughout his letters. In Romans 6:3-4, for instance, he compares being baptized to dying and rising with Christ. Baptism is incorporation into the body of Christ, the way we become part of the people of God. The water is used to symbolize the fact that, in this act, God changes our status, cleanses us, justifies us, and receives us as citizens of his kingdom.

Those who are baptized as adults are called upon to acknowledge what this act means to them. Publicly, they declare their sin and their faith, and promise to live in an intimate relationship with God. This is necessary because their baptism marks a distinct change from the past. They are conscious of a new form of life opening up before them. Those who are baptized as infants make no such declaration because they have no awareness of the significance of the act.

ROMANS 12:1-8

With eyes wide open to the mercies of God, I beg you, my brothers, as an act of intelligent worship, to give him your bodies, as a living sacrifice, consecrated to him and acceptable by him. Don't let the world around you squeeze you into its own mold, but let God remold your minds from within, so that you may prove in practice that the plan of God for you is good, meets all his demands and moves toward the goal of true maturity.

As your spiritual teacher I give this piece of advice to each one of you. Don't cherish exaggerated ideas of yourself or your importance, but try to have a sane estimate of your capabilities by the light of the faith that God has given to you all. For just as you have many members in one physical body and those members differ in their functions, so we, though many in number, compose one body in Christ and are all members of one another. Through the grace of God we have different gifts. If our gift is preaching, let us preach to the limit of our vision. If it is serving others let us concentrate on our service; if it is teaching let us give all we have to our teaching; and if our gift be the stimulating of the faith of others let us set ourselves to it. Let the man who is called to give, give freely; let the man who wields authority think of his responsibility; and let the man who feels sympathy for his fellows act cheerfully.

— J. B. Phillips

The practice of infant baptism is further evidence that we take the grace of God seriously. If we believe that God's grace is his free gift of himself, then we believe that God gives himself fully even to those of his people who cannot respond to it intellectually. Yet human freedom of decision is preserved. As the baptized baby matures, he can consciously accept or reject God's grace by his own choice. It is the purpose and the duty of the congregation's program of Christian education to help him understand what this choice means to his life. For this reason, our church has adopted the program of catechetical instruction and has used a special rite of confirmation.

Confirmation is the church's way of acknowledging the youth's growing maturity and capacity to decide for himself where he stands in his membership in the people of God. The rite confirms the church's acceptance of the youth as one who is now ready to assume more responsibility in working together with his fellow Christians to carry out the church's mission. Confirmation also reminds the youth of God's lasting baptismal gifts.

THE LORD'S SUPPER OR HOLY COMMUNION

The other sacrament, the Lord's Supper or Holy Communion, reminds us of the Upper Room in Jerusalem on the night before Jesus died. As we share bread and wine at the altar, we hear his words, "Take, eat; this is my Body, which is given for you. . . . Drink ye all of it; this cup is the new testament in my Blood, which is shed for you. . . ." As we eat the bread and drink the wine, following the example of the first disciples, Christ comes to each of us in a marvelous way. In his sacrament, God gives us his assurance that he comes to us in the living presence of Christ, forgiving our sin and strengthening us for daily consecrated living with him.

Holy Communion is the church's central act of worship because in it we participate in personal fellowship with the risen Christ and with each other in a memorable way. As Christians, we therefore "celebrate" Holy Communion. It is not a sad service but a thankful, joyous gathering of Christians to celebrate the mighty act of God in Christ which is renewed again and again as we commune with him.

WORD AND SACRAMENTS

As the people of God, we need the Word and the sacraments to link us with God, to bring his message to us. Together, they are the means of grace, the ways by which his gifts of love pour into us.

Our relationship with the church hinges upon God's Word, and that relationship needs continual nourishment by the means of grace. Notice how the Constitution of the Lutheran Church in America centers the life of the church upon the gospel, the Word of God:

This Church affirms that the Gospel transmitted by the Holy Scriptures, to which the creeds and confessions bear witness, is the true treasure of the Church, the substance of its proclamation, and the basis of its unity and continuity. The Holy Spirit uses the proclamation of the Gospel and the administration of the Sacraments to create and sustain Christian faith and fellowship. As this occurs, the Church fulfills its divine mission and purpose.

—LCA Constitution, Article II, Section 7

O Lord God, great trouble has come upon me. My cares overwhelm me; I know not where to turn. God, be gracious to me and help me. Give me strength to bear what thou sendest and let not fear rule over me. Provide like a father for those I love. Merciful Father, forgive all my sins against thee and against men. I trust thy grace and commit my life to thy hands. Do with me what thou wilt and what is good for me. Whether I live or die, I am with thee and thou with me, my God. Lord, I wait for thy salvation and for thy kingdom. Amen.

—DIETRICH BONHOEFFER

6

UNDERSTANDING THE BIBLE

FEW people would attempt to build a house without first consulting building plans and blueprints prepared by experts. Of course, you could put together some kind of house working on your own, but it is doubtful that you would be fully satisfied with the results. Most of us turn to reliable sources of knowledge and experience when we undertake anything of importance. Should this be any less true when we are thinking of our relationship to God and the Christian life? Fortunately, we have a source book, the Bible, which gives us the benefit of the experience and knowledge of many people who lived closely with God over thousands of years.

CHARACTERISTICS

We believe that the Bible is revealed truth. Revelation is a term we use to describe God's disclosure of himself to man. In using it, we distinguish between general and special revelation. When we speak of revelation as being *general* or *natural,* we are referring to God's disclosure of himself in the natural world. Properly speaking, general revelation comes through the discoveries of science as well as through the awe we feel in the presence of God's wonders in nature. We use the term *special* revelation to refer to God's revelation of himself through events of history as interpreted by inspired men.

We believe that because of special revelation, the Bible is inspired. Inspiration is a gift of special understanding and insight by which some persons recognize the activity of God in history and interpret its meaning for others. In the biblical sense, inspiration does not raise a man above the limitations imposed by his own weaknesses or by his particular time and place in history. Each biblical writer therefore expresses his thoughts in contemporary language and images shaped by his own personal experiences. What he produces can be said to be inspired to the extent that he himself is inspired. It is in this sense that we speak of the Bible as an inspired book.

The Bible offers considerable variety in the ways God's people through the years have understood their relationship with God. The actual writing and assembling of the Bible covers several thousand years, and its subject matter an even longer span. Therefore, we should not be surprised that there is such a wide variety in both its expression of general knowledge and its perception of special revelation. In some of the early passages, the biblical writers use rather primitive forms of expression, reflecting the tribal culture of the time. Portions of the New Testament, on the other hand, use language and concepts which were meaningful in the relatively high culture of classical Greece and Rome. At each stage of this long process of growth, the message of the Bible is transmitted through the thought-forms and cultural expressions native to the authors.

Paul, the product of both Jewish and Greek education, writing in the first century A.D., expressed his understanding of God at work in the world in different terms from those used by the prophet Amos, a simple shepherd of the eighth century B.C. Similarly, if you felt inspired to sit down and write your thoughts about God today, it would be reasonable to expect that you might do so in quite different terms than either Amos or Paul, although the basic truth you express might be the same.

The Bible offers additional variety in the many kinds of writings collected in its pages. It is a virtual library of histories, letters, stories, dramas, poetry, memoirs, prophecies. That is why most people who try to read it from beginning to end in the sequence in which it is assembled are disappointed and confused. The writers of the Scriptures not only made use of words and illustrations current at the times they were writing, but they also employed a variety of literary forms, such as sermons and oracles, parables and similies, wise maxims and strange visions. Each book of the Bible was written for a specific purpose. In some instances the exact purpose of some books is now obscure. However, for the most part, we know in general why the various books were prepared. Many of them were written primarily to help the faithful understand and survive a crisis, such as invasion of their country or persecution or the appearance of false teachers in their midst. If you want to understand the message of a book of the Bible, it is helpful to begin by determining what kind of literature it is and why the author used that particular literary form.

Basically, the Bible is a book of religion. It recounts events and the interpretation of events in which God reveals himself; it relates his attitude of love toward his people and his expectations of them. The Bible is not a textbook of science, astronomy, or geography. Although it contains history, it is not a history book. Although there are many colorful stories, it was not designed to entertain. First and foremost, the Bible was designed to confront men with God.

THE BIBLE AND SCIENCE

Christians, like all human beings, have a normal share of curiosity about the origin and nature of the universe. Christians believe that God in some wonderful fashion created the universe and that he continues to care for it. At times, however, curiosity about the universe and faith in God have produced tensions. This is especially true in the light of man's scientific discoveries.

Take the discoveries of Copernicus, for example. Copernicus revolutionized thinking with his discovery that the earth was not flat but a sphere that revolved around the sun. It seemed quite impossible for Christians to believe that the sun was the center of their universe when both the evidence of their senses and Holy Scriptures seemed to indicate quite clearly that the earth was the hub of the universe. "How could God have commanded the sun to stand still for Joshua if it does not move around the earth?" asked the literal-minded. Much later the publication of Darwin's *The Origin of Species* set off a tremendous furor among Christians who thought that the suggestion that man evolved from lower forms of life was a contradiction of the biblical account of creation. Paul Scherer once told a story to illustrate an unfortunate state of mind which sometimes plagues Christians. In the twenties, the right to teach the theory of evolution in the public schools was contested in the Tennessee courts. Nationwide attention was focused on the "Scopes' Monkey" trial and the legal battle between William Jennings Bryan for the prosecution and Clarence Darrow for the defense. According to Scherer, a pious little old lady who lived in the town where the trial took place was overheard at her prayers one night: "O Lord, may it not be true that men are descended from the apes; but, O Lord, if it should turn out to be true, please, Lord, do not let it become widely known."

A curious mixture of piety, fundamentalism, literalism, and pride among the people of God has bothered the church for centuries as it has grappled with the problem of relating revealed truth to man's ever-growing knowledge about himself and his world. On one side there are Christians who sincerely feel that acceptance of the Bible as the inspired Word of God requires them to reject any discovery or view that seems to contradict any part of the sacred writing. On the other side, there are many who accept the findings of science without reservation and believe that since the Bible appears to be unalterably anchored to an archaic, three-decker world view, it is no longer to be trusted in any respect. Both attitudes are unwarranted and unnecessary extremes.

THE CHRISTIAN'S ANSWER

Robert Marshall helps us develop a sound and sensible Christian world view:

> Like the ancient Hebrew writer, today's believer also lives in a culture that has its own way of describing the origin of the world. Must a Christian then possess a world view different from that of everyone else? The answer would seem to be both "Yes" and "No." Some kinds of knowledge come by human investigation. Here science has proved its worth, and even where scientific thought must remain quite theoretical, the believer must not go out of his way to pick a quarrel. Time schedules, the processes of nature, and a good many other things are not matters of faith or revelation. Consequently, the biblical author held views similar to those of neighboring people who did not worship his God, and the modern Christian has no more light on many topics than science is able to provide. On the other hand, faith and revelation have to do with God and man's relationship with God. These are the subjects on which not the scientist, but the Bible writer and the Christian believer have something distinctive to say.*

Let us probe this matter further by dealing with specifics. Read the first two chapters of Genesis, which deal with the process of creation. First of all, we must ask about the literary forms used and the purpose for which they were written.

When you read these chapters carefully, you will notice that there are really two Creation stories here. The main characters are the same, but the sequence of events and the details vary. One story probably paralleled an ancient folktale which had some currency in several of the countries around Israel. The second story, which includes a more detailed account of the creation of man and woman, contains

* Robert J. Marshall, *The Mighty Acts of God* (Philadelphia: Lutheran Church Press, 1964), pp. 26-27.

some material which has led biblical scholars to conclude that it was used by the Hebrew priests in their teaching.

It is a generally accepted conclusion that the Book of Genesis, along with Exodus, Leviticus, Numbers, and Deuteronomy, was incorporated into the body of Jewish scriptures fairly late, probably as a part of a reformation movement in the seventh century B.C. Although much of the material in these books had existed for hundreds of years as part of an accumulating oral tradition, it took a long time for it to be given the status of Scripture. One conjecture is that these oral traditions were written down specifically to undergird the reformation movement.

The authors of the Creation accounts do not pretend to have been eyewitnesses to the act of creation, a claim which would have sounded as absurd to them as it does to us. They were aware that they neither knew how or when creation took place. What they did know was that God was responsible for all existence And the ancient folklore they report includes some remarkably accurate observations about the nature of things. For instance, the day-by-day description of creation in Genesis 1 is very close to the stages scientists postulate in the formation and development of the world. However, the authors' purpose was not scientific analysis. "In the beginning God" (Genesis 1:1) is not a description of the start of calendar time but an assertion that God is before, over, and responsible for all that is. The poetic symbolism of six days of creative activity supports the conviction that creation did not occur instantaneously but that there was an orderly progression over a period of time.

There are three important implications in the biblical accounts of Creation that should be explored. The accounts affirm that God is Lord of all life, that God is sovereign. This is another way of saying that creation was not accidental, but purposeful, orderly, law-abiding, and intelligible. This understanding does not rule out acceptance of theories of biological evolution. Science describes the "how" of creation; the Bible describes the "why." Other sections of the Bible, such as Job 38—41 and Isaiah 40—66, echo this belief in the lordship of God the Creator.

The accounts also affirm that creation is continuous. Here, traditional Christian belief and some schools of modern science are in agreement, although they do not use identical language to describe their common convictions. Christians believe that God is still involved with his creation, sustaining, controlling, and furthering it. Scientists recognize that the ongoing process of creativity in the universe is guided by principles and processes to make changes inevitable.

The accounts, lastly, affirm that creation is good. After each stage of creation, Genesis comments "And God saw that it was good." This means that matter itself is good. It is man who decides whether to use matter for good or for evil. He can collect rocks to build a house; he can use a rock to kill another person. Jesus took bread and wine and used them in the sacrament of Holy Communion to convey the most profound spiritual blessings. The gifts of bread and wine can be abused by overeating and drunkenness. Another proof that material things are good is implied in the doctrine of incarnation. Some of the world's religions teach that the human body is evil, but not Christianity. The body is part of the whole man and the whole man is loved by God.

Therefore, as Christians we are under no constraint to escape from this material world, to mortify our flesh and glorify our spirits. Instead, Christianity offers us a way of working constructively and positively among the commonplace "things" of creation.

Even though man can and often does warp and distort matter and use it in evil ways, Christians still insist that greater harm is done by valuing material things too little. In a spirit of thankfulness, Christians feel they should use the things of the world wisely and well. The Christian therefore should have a strong sense of stewardship. From brushing teeth to reforestation, from shining shoes to conserving natural wonders, the Christian has an impulse to preserve and value worldly things. For this reason, we support scientific investigation to discover better ways in which we can serve as stewards of all that God has made. Every advance in the battles against cancer and heart disease, every development in making farmland more productive, every new advancement in human knowledge is cause for rejoicing.

In the last few years, the Creation stories have taken on new relevance as man moves out from his earth to explore the moon and neighboring planets. No one knows how far man will penetrate the vastness of the universe nor what he will find. But whatever discoveries are in store for us, we will welcome them as new avenues for intelligent and joyful stewardship of God's gifts, and as new domains in which Christ is Savior and over which he is Lord.

The procedure we have followed in discussing the Creation stories is a useful guide for your study of all parts of the Bible's message. Consult Bible dictionaries and commentaries for background information about literary forms and the purpose of the various writings and then approach them knowledgeably and reflectively. In this way, the Word of God can come to be a meaningful guide for daily living.

REFLECTIONS ABOUT TIME

There are several biblical concepts that we should consider because understanding their usage is helpful in probing the insights that the biblical books have to offer. One such concept is time.

There are many ways to think about time. We usually think of it as a chronological movement. All of our devices for measuring time foster this idea—sun dials, water clocks, wristwatches. The hands on your watch move and their movement seems to measure the passing of time. When time is viewed as chronology, it is quite natural to think of it as having a beginning and eventually an end. Everything we know in life can be measured by its beginning and its ending, its birth and its death. The Bible also speaks of chronological or passing time. The ancient Hebrews had no watches or electric clocks with which to measure time, but they counted the days and hours in their own way with reasonable accuracy. They were as soberly aware that life has a beginning and an end as we are. It was likewise as easy for them as it is for us to assume that the universe itself had a similar terminal point. This linear concept of time is useful and reasonably uncomplicated until we consider the concept of eternity. Then all sorts of complications arise because the human mind simply cannot grasp, in any meaningful way, an absolutely endless flow of time. The biblical authors had as much difficulty as we do in attempting to comprehend an eternal God who confers eternal life upon believers. Even Paul struggled to develop a way of expressing the Christian concept of eternity to men who are, in mind and body, prisoners of chronological time.

Those who produced the Scriptures came to a fairly satisfactory solution by pointing out that even though God acts within chronological time, he transcends time simply because he is God. The Letter of James speaks of God "with whom there is no variation or shadow due to change" (1:17). The Letter to the Hebrews exalts Christ "the same yesterday and today and for ever" (13:8). Maybe the best way for us to grasp the meaning of the quality of eternalness would be to reverse our usual idea that time is passing and consciously remind ourselves that it is we who are passing; it is the universe that is passing, while time itself neither grows old nor dies. If our thoughts of God could be related to that sort of time concept, we would not be troubled by such questions as "How can God know all about me—past, present, and even the future which has not yet happened in chronological time?" The answer is that God can do this because he is not limited to chronological time. There is a rough illustration of this phenomenon in the experience we call a dream. According to some experts, a dream usually lasts only a few seconds, even though the experience dreamed about may cover a span of hours, days, or even years. It may even seem to us that we have been dreaming for hours. Another part of the dream experience is the dreamer's feeling that he is both watching what happens in a dream sequence as well as participating in it. Time and space in a dream are quite different from our understanding of reality. God similarly transcends our human limitations and knows of time in different dimensions.

IMMORTALITY OR ETERNAL LIFE

Jesus taught that a new age, a new way of noting divisions in time, had begun with him. However, he almost certainly did not mean that the old age had abruptly and completely ended—at least, not in a chronological sense. What he did mean was that a new dimension of meaning had been added to the world, that new possibilities had opened for man. The new dimension was clearly relevant to chronological time because Jesus expected man to be able to recognize and enjoy it; but, just as clearly, it transcended chronological time. Christians believe that this new dimension is what the New Testament means by "eternal life." Eternal life begins not after death but when, through faith, a person is incorporated into the people of God. He still participates fully in chronological time but, at the same time, he is part of another dimensional time relationship.

Martin J. Heinecken explains this concept:

Those who have heard the word of reconciliation have already entered into a new life. They have "eternal life," that is, they have that new quality of life which is no longer subject to death. For them, the years that separate them from the cross and Resurrection of Christ vanish, and they become "contemporary" with those events. They have been buried with Christ into his death and all their sins with them; and they have been raised with him to newness of life.*

* Martin J. Heinecken, *The Beginning and End of the World* (Philadelphia: Muhlenberg Press, 1960), pp. 32-33.

LIFE AFTER DEATH

It is virtually impossible for us not to wonder what will happen to us after we die. Ever since men first learned to think, they have probed this question with every resource at their command. They have sought answers in the mystical signs of nature and in their own careful reasoning. They have produced theories of life after death that fitted in with their own style of living. Some anthropologists classify this universal desire to continue living in an afterlife as a kind of wishful thinking that helps make this life bearable.

Christians share a concern for life after death with the rest of humanity, but with one important difference. Christians believe that the Creator God who has revealed himself to be a God of love is to be trusted. He has promised to do what is best for his people after death as he does during their lives. Through Christ, God revealed his plan to offer his people a continuation of their life with him beyond death. Because God raised Jesus from the dead, he promises the same resurrection from the dead in a new form of life to all believers. This is the power of the gospel that John expressed succinctly: "God so loved the world that he gave his only son, that whoever believes in him should not perish but have everlasting life" (John 3:16).

It is rather pointless to speculate on the details of eternal life. We only know what Christ has told us, and he was more interested in helping us learn to live with God now than in focusing our attention on the future. Eternal life really begins when we accept God as our Lord. As Christians, we learn the joy of living with God in trust and hope. This is all we need for successful living both now and in the life to come. With God's help, we strengthen our trust in him. He brought Christ from the dead and for our sakes conquered death.

HEAVEN AND HELL

In our sophisticated age, people are inclined to dispense with such seemingly naive ideas as heaven and hell, to discard them as relics of a superstitious age now long gone. However, the ideas of heaven and hell are still meaningful if we can prevent a biblical literalism from obscuring them.

It is hard to dispel traditional thinking about heaven and hell as geographical places. Both the Bible and the liturgies of the church have many familiar references to their location. A literal interpretation of these terms has little relevance in our understanding of the universe. But this should not be our interpretation—any more than it was in the Creation stories. Inability to locate heaven and hell geographically by no means cancels the truths they are intended to convey. As a matter of fact, removing them from space and time makes them more meaningful. Quite simply, heaven describes a state of fellowship with God and hell is the absence of it. Both are matters of experience here and now. Extended, heaven becomes a synonym for the gift of eternal life and hell a synonym for eternal death.

THE END OF THE WORLD

A third area of general biblical concern that commands our attention is the end of the world. This is also a subject for speculation today. Scientists feel that the world will perhaps come to an end by some cosmic accident or by a change in the sun. The world could end by man's design in a fiery holocaust of nuclear destruction. Christianity accepts the fact of an eventual world's end because it is part of God's plan. However, there is a deep concern for preventing its destruction by man's design before God has fulfilled his purposes. The primary concern and expectation expressed by men of faith in the Bible is centered on the end of the world and of man in this sense of fulfillment. The Bible assumes that creation has a purpose and that God directs it toward the end or goal of realizing that purpose. Therefore, as Christians we accept the inevitable end of the world as the fulfillment of God's purpose as he draws all things unto himself creating the fullness of his kingdom.

THE SECOND COMING OF CHRIST

Traditionally, the church believes in the second coming of Christ, which is connected with the end of the world and a foretold Day of Judgment. It is admittedly difficult to understand precisely what is meant by New Testament references to this event. The references are scant and are intermingled with wishful hopes. According to the New Testament records, the earliest Christians expected Jesus to return again very soon. When he did not appear, the "soon" was changed to "later" and has now stretched out to almost twenty centuries. The Gospel writers reported Jesus' promises that he would return; but his statements, as we now have them, are ambiguous. The best way to consider his second coming is in terms of the biblical concept of time which we have already discussed. Remember that human sense of time as chronology doesn't fit God's view of the world. He is over and above our sequence of events. The New Testament frequently uses the Greek word *kairos* to describe this other dimension of time. *Kairos* is better translated as "the right or critical time," a situation which is filled with decisive opportunities for man, a situation in which God is performing his judging and healing work. Christ came in such a moment of time for his work of redemption heralding the kingdom of God. It was probably in the context of *kairos* that Christ spoke of his second coming.

We know that Christ is a judging factor in history as he is in our individual lives. In that sense, at least, every day is Judgment Day. Then, too, he comes to us daily as we open our hearts to receive him as our Lord. These facts of experience combine with the biblical witness to keep the expectation alive and real that Christ will one day gather all the people of God into the kingdom without end.

O God, give us courage—courage to make experiments, and not to be afraid of making mistakes; courage to get up when we are down; courage to work with all our might for the coming of thy kingdom on earth; through Jesus Christ our Lord. Amen. —AUTHOR UNKNOWN

O Lord, Shield of Our Help, who wilt not suffer us to be tempted above that we are able, help us, we entreat thee, in all our straits and wrestlings, to lift up our eyes unto thee, and stay our hearts on thee; through Jesus Christ. Amen. —CHRISTINA GEORGINA ROSSETTI

7

the church's ministry

THE direction of Christianity is always from God to man. It is God's way of dealing with his people. The center of Christianity, the incarnation, is ample evidence that God is active in the world. And man, the particular focus of God's fatherly concern, can be a son of the divine household, heir to the fullness of grace, and the ambassador of his Father to his world. United with fellow believers in the fellowship of the people of God, the Christian shares in the church's ministry to all levels and areas of society. This ministry is empowered by God himself. This presence of God within his church, guiding it to perform its tasks, we call the Holy Spirit.

GOD THE HOLY SPIRIT

In our creeds, we confess our faith in the Holy Spirit. We use this term to designate the way God works in human history. Unfortunately, the doctrine of the Holy Spirit has often been misinterpreted, especially when the old English synonym, Holy Ghost, is used. Yet it is very helpful in understanding the nature and power of God.

The Holy Spirit came to men as a fulfillment of Christ's promise. Just before the Lord ascended, he said to his followers: "I will pray the Father, and he will give you another

Counselor, to be with you for ever, even the Spirit of truth . . ." (John 14:16-17). A short time later, when the disciples were gathered together, the Holy Spirit was in the midst of them and they knew what Jesus meant. Luke describes the event:

> And suddenly a sound came from heaven like the rush of a mighty wind, and it filled all the house where they were sitting. And there appeared to them tongues as of fire, distributed and resting on each one of them. And they were all filled with the Holy Spirit and began to speak in other tongues, as the Spirit gave them utterance.
>
> *—Acts 2:2-4*

This was not the first time the Holy Spirit had come into the world. According to one of the writers of Genesis, the work of creation is ascribed to the Spirit of God: "The Spirit of God was moving over the face of the waters" (1:2). All through the Old Testament there is an expressed consciousness of the operation of the Spirit of God in the lives of God's people. The Holy Spirit is much in evidence in the events connected with the birth and baptism of Jesus, according to the Gospels. Jesus often talked about the Holy Spirit in his teaching sessions. Understanding God as the Holy Spirit and accepting his work in his world is part of the Christian faith.

THE HOLY TRINITY

Before we explore the Spirit's work in nurturing the church, perhaps we should pause to consider the Christian idea of God as the Holy Trinity. The Bible makes it quite clear that God has revealed himself in three ways: as God the Father, the Creator; as God the Son, the Redeemer; and as God the Holy Spirit, the Sanctifier. The church tries to express this experience through the term the Holy Trinity. By this the church means that there is one God whom we know as three persons. This can easily sound confusing because we think of a person as a separate and distinct entity, an "I." But the original word which we translate as person did not have the connotation which it does for us. It meant originally, the mask worn by an actor, and hence is more akin to "aspect" or "role." The three-person idea was related to the threefold nature of God. The mystery of God is far beyond the capacity of the human mind to explain. We can only interpret him as we know him through his revelation of himself, in terms of his actions on our behalf. The Trinitarian expression of faith in the threefold nature of God corresponds with the three ways that we experience him: as Creator and Father in the vastness of creation; as Son in the redeeming work of Christ; and as Holy Spirit moving his church on its mission through the centuries.

There is a fine book about Luther's teachings entitled *Let God Be God*. That title is a good slogan. In our relationships with him, we have to acknowledge the fact that he is God. If there are mysteries and unfathomable depths, we can only marvel. Accepting God as our God is to come before him with a sense of awe. Even Paul, the church's greatest theologian, found moments when he could only say:

O the depth of the riches and wisdom and knowledge of God! How unsearchable are his judgments and how inscrutable his ways!
    "For who has known the mind of the Lord,
    or who has been his counselor?"
    "Or who has given a gift to him
    that he might be repaid?"
For from him and through him and to him are all things.
To him be glory forever. Amen.   —*Romans 11:33-36*

"For from him and through him and to him are all things" is a healthy reminder of the only perspective from which we can gain a dependable view of what life really means and who we really are as persons. We come to understand our own individual stature best when we see ourselves as functional members of God's family. He is always in the midst of his people as the Holy Spirit—guiding them, reproving them, strengthening them.

PENTECOST

As you read Luke's description of what happened on Pentecost (Acts 2), you will note the ways he tried to express an inexpressible experience of the Spirit's coming to the little band of Jesus' followers. The only thing Luke could do was to use comparisons: There was a sound "like the rush of a mighty wind"; the disciples and others who were there experienced a strange sensation like "tongues as of fire, distributed and resting on each one of them." Both of Luke's comparisons are good choices to help us understand the phenomenon of God the Holy Spirit in our presence. You cannot see the wind, but you know it is there. You can feel it, and you can see its effects as it bends trees and makes the leaves rustle. This is a good way to describe the presence and actions of God in our world.

Fire, too, is an apt illustration of the Spirit's power. We speak of someone who is enthusiastic about some cause as being "on fire." The Spirit gives his people the fire to turn their convictions into courses of action.

Read the Pentecost story in Acts 2. This is an excellent starting point for considering the Spirit's work. What God did for that early church he does for all his people when they open themselves to his influence.

It will be helpful to examine the gifts of the Holy Spirit as he inspires the church's ministry.

FELLOWSHIP

The Book of Acts, which is really a report of the young church in action, offers many references to the unique sense of fellowship among the first Christians. One early critic of the church pointed to the mutual concern demonstrated by Christians as one of their most remarkable and noticeable characteristics. Indeed, a profound sense of community among the disciples was one of the first visible effects of Pentecost, an effect which was extended to others as they became followers of Christ. We still value fellowship as one of the prime expressions of the Christian faith. Usually, the effectiveness of the church membership can be measured in direct ratio to the experience of true fellowship.

Some people may react negatively to the word fellowship. Unfortunately, in common usage fellowship includes everything from shallow, back-slapping "get-togethers" to genuine interpersonal relationships. The New Testament prefers to use the Greek word *koinonia*. *Koinonia* is strong fellowship with mutual respect and concern among those who share it.

The depth of this fellowship in the early church is vividly illustrated by the closeness of its members, which lead them to share their worldly possessions with each other:

> Now the company of those who believed were of one heart and soul, and no one said that any of the things which he possessed was his own, but they had everything in common. . . . There was not a needy person among them, for as many as were possessors of lands or houses sold them, and brought the proceeds of what was sold and laid it at the apostles' feet; and distribution was made to each as any had need.　　　　　*—Acts 4:32-35*

Paul must have had this sort of mutual dependence and support in mind when he used the phrase "the body of Christ" as a description of the church. As Paul rightly understood the fellowship, it has meaning for the people of God only if they are first linked in fellowship with Christ. Jesus used an apt illustration of this fellowship in his allegory of the vine and the branches:

> "I am the vine, you are the branches. He who abides in me, and I in him, he it is that bears much fruit, for apart from me you can do nothing."　　　　　*—John 15:5*

Through the power of the Holy Spirit working through the fellowship of God's people, the church is able to carry out its ministry. Basically, this ministry has two functions: nurture and outreach.

THE CHURCH'S MINISTRY OF NURTURE

The church's ministry of nurture involves caring for the spiritual growth of its members. It is concerned with the healthy development of the church family. This is not unlike the necessity we have to care for our physical health. Our ability to do our jobs, as well as our sense of well-being, depends on it.

The existence of sin prevents the fellowship from reaching perfection. For this reason, the church is always under obligation to build itself up—feeding the members of the body, healing their wounds, nourishing their faith, and, in general, equipping them for service to their world. The ministry of nurture includes many functions and activities in the life of the local congregation.

WORSHIP

Public worship is a regular part of the congregation's life. It is essential for the congregation's health.

The reason for this is quite plain. The Service confronts the worshipers with the Word and the sacraments. At the same time, worship is an expression of the basic fellowship of the congregation. In addition, the church guides its people in cultivating regular habits of personal and family worship. Though worship is basically a ministry of the church to its members, an invitation is always extended to nonmembers to share in this meeting with God.

Faithful participation in both public and private worship is an essential part of your church life. The worship section of this book provides you with a number of aids to help you build a meaningful worship life.

CHRISTIAN EDUCATION

The church has traditionally placed a strong emphasis upon education. People are always growing and changing. They continually need guidance in applying God's truths to their lives. A recent slogan for parish education month was "As long as you live, you learn; as long as you learn, you live." The Parish Education Curriculum of the Lutheran Church in America is designed as a comprehensive and flexible series of courses for people of all ages. Most congregations provide a variety of educational opportunities to meet the needs and interests of their members. There are many courses, for example, which offer deeper study of themes introduced in this course. No member of the church should neglect his responsibility to cultivate his understanding of the Christian faith. Only by sound study and careful thinking can we keep ourselves attuned to the Holy Spirit's guidance.

STEWARDSHIP

Both the worship life of the congregation and its educational enterprises groom church members for leadership roles. Everyone has talents to serve his fellow Christians in some leadership capacity if he is willing to serve with commitment and determination. Christians owe this to their Lord and his church as a joyful response to all the gifts God gives them freely from his great love.

Response through service is called "stewardship." The church uses this term to refer to all the ways in which we use our gifts wisely—whether it be talents, money, or time. Wisdom, in the Christian sense, means living with such a thankful spirit that you are willing to use your resources to serve God and your fellowmen.

One avenue of response through service is by giving gifts of money to the church's work. However, never forget that stewardship extends far beyond the giving of money. It includes the care and proper use of all that God has entrusted to you in terms of time (all the hours and days that comprise your life on earth), talents (all the ability and gifts that make it possible to earn a living and to enjoy it), and money (a symbol or token of all your material resources).

The Christian's stewardship response determines to a large part how far and how well the church can carry out its ministry. There is no use pretending the church doesn't need money; it does. And it has no source of income except the generosity of its members. As a member of a congregation, you are naturally and properly concerned about its budgets—its income and the use of its income. However, if you interpret your stewardship only in terms of local concerns, the chances are that you will have a very narrow view of the church. In the final analysis, what you give to the work of the church should be determined not by the congregation's budget but by your sensitivity to the love of God in Christ. Nothing can motivate you sufficiently to practice genuine Christian stewardship except a deep thankfulness for the life, death, and resurrection of Christ and their meaning for your spiritual growth. In The Service, the Lutheran church links the offering of the church with the preparation of the elements to be used in Communion. This arrangement symbolizes the commitment and dedication of the whole of life to God in response to his matchless gifts of deliverance, forgiveness, and eternal life.

Developing a keen sense of stewardship is a hard task at times because we are so accustomed to thinking that all we have belongs to us, that no one else, however worthy, has any right to it. With this kind of comfortable attitude, we tend to give to good causes only what we feel we can spare from our surplus funds. The Christian, though, begins to see that this point of view is somewhat twisted. Really, all that we have comes from God. Therefore, our gifts to him are simply returning, with our good wishes, what already belongs to him.

> We give thee but thine own,
> Whate'er the gift may be;
> All that we have is thine alone,
> A trust, O Lord, from thee.
> SBH 544

THE PASTOR

Because the church's ministry of nurture is so extensive and complex, the congregation calls some qualified Christian to serve as pastor and minister in the name of the congregation to the needs of its people.

Most people have a well-fixed mental image of what a pastor is like and what he does. These images range from a well-intentioned but ineffectual religious professional to a pious person who is elevated above common humanity.

Your concept of the pastor and his role has an influence on your relationship to the congregation. Therefore, it is important to know exactly who the pastor is and what he does for each of us in our church fellowship.

First of all, never forget that the pastor is human. His ordination has not elevated him to another plane of existence. Being human, he has essentially the same desires and feelings, and is subject to the same temptations, as all mankind. He needs and receives the grace of God like everyone else. He neither is nor claims to be infallible in his interpretation of the Bible. But he is a man who has dedicated his life to helping guide the spiritual life of God's people. The church emphasizes the significance of the pastor through its stress on his call to the ministry, his substantial training and education, his ordination, and his installation. All of this expresses the respect in which the church holds the office of pastor. This respect is real and deserved, as an examination of the pastor's work demonstrates.

SHEPHERD OF THE FLOCK

The term pastor means shepherd, the keeper of the flock. This is a good description of the unique relationship of the pastor to the congregation. Lutherans customarily call their minister "pastor" rather than preacher or parson or reverend, because this title best suggests the whole range of ways in which he serves them. In biblical terms a shepherd was a responsible guardian of the sheep in his care. He was responsible for guiding them in such a way that they would be nurtured and preserved in the face of danger.

So close and protecting was the relationship of the shepherd to his flock, that the psalmist used it as a metaphor to describe his relationship with God: "The LORD is my shepherd, I shall not want" (Psalm 23:1). Later, Jesus used the term to identify his ministry with God's concern for his world: "I am the good shepherd. The good shepherd lays down his life for the sheep" (John 10:11).

The pastor is trained and called to serve with the idea that his chief function is to minister to the needs of the congregation and its members. For that purpose, he is equipped by education in college and seminary to preach and teach the Word of God, to exercise a ministry of healing and consolation, to help people realize their potential as God's family. In these functions he is expected to be something of an expert and to apply himself to his duties with diligence and commitment. While the pastor may be called upon to assume other duties, he must deal with these concerns first.

While it is true that worship, religious education, and the "care of souls" are all essential for the well-being of the congregation and its members, the maintenance of this well-being has a purpose, and this purpose is the ministry of outreach. The congregation is gathered by the Holy Spirit, created continuously by the Word of God, for a purpose: to proclaim the kingdom of God.

THE MINISTRY OF OUTREACH

One of the revitalizing factors in the life of the church today is the realization that the nurture of the community of faith is not an end in itself. Simply being nurtured in the Christian faith is not enough. We also need to participate in the vast mission of the church beyond the boundaries of congregational life. God did not create his church to be a mutual admiration society but to be the agent of the Holy Spirit proclaiming the good news of Christ to the world.

Neither pastors nor congregations would be likely to forget the true mission of the church if they took the Pentecost story seriously. One effect of the Holy Spirit's visitation on that memorable day was the endowment of the disciples with the ability and desire to proclaim the gospel. The "speaking in tongues" that they manifested was symbolic of their newfound ability to communicate the gospel so clearly and convincingly that it was good news in any language. Peter's vigorous Pentecost sermon (Acts 2:14-36) indicated that his understanding of the Old Testament Scriptures had been given a new and exciting dimension by his experiences with Christ and his inspiration by the Holy Spirit. The power of the gospel that Peter preached changed people because it spoke to their needs. The message had relevance and challenge. It is significant that one of the first acts of this specially called fellowship of believers was to preach the good news of God.

From its very beginning the infant church accepted the proclamation of the gospel as one of its chief functions. The New Testament uses the Greek word *kerygma* to describe this proclamation. It is translated as "preaching," but it means more than preaching: It apparently includes any sort of activity that constitutes an announcement of God's mighty act in Christ. Many changes have taken place in the world since the gospel was first preached; but the gospel remains the same, and God's mandate to proclaim it still exists. The church's task today is to translate the gospel into terms that modern men can understand, so they can see how it meets their deepest needs.

THE GOSPEL AND MAN TODAY

We know that modern life tends to depersonalize man. Urban living, automation, and the growing institutionalization of life all conspire to rob man of status, dignity, and meaning. Each person needs to know that despite these forces he is an individual of worth created in God's image. Right in the midst of these depersonalizing forces, Jesus Christ redeems him and makes him part of the fellowship of the gospel.

This is a changing world. Changes are rapid and radical. Every day poses new problems and crises for men to face. Consider the effects of population mobility, the paradox of coexisting plenty and poverty, the growth of giant power blocs and organizations. The church is equipped to bring the light of the gospel to bear in these and other areas where man is in difficulty, so that it can help them find themselves in their time of need.

MINISTRY, INDIVIDUAL AND SOCIAL

The foundation of the early church's proclamation of the gospel was the power of the message itself together with a powerful sense of community. Those first Christians formed a remarkable community of unusual depth and meaning; they practiced what they preached and were, in a sense, living gospels to the world. In their helping and strengthening each other, they developed a keener understanding of service. The Greek word they used to describe this ministry is *diakonia*, which we usually translate as "service" but which also includes dimensions of reconciliation and healing. Generally, this concept of service applies to those who have special responsibilities in the church, such as church councilmen, deacons, elders, and deaconesses (the word deacon comes from *diakonia*). However, all members of the Christian community are called to serve each other as well as those outside their group.

Jesus gave us an excellent example of *diakonia* in his famous Parable of the Good Samaritan (Luke 10:29-37). Jesus told the story in answer to a young lawyer's question about inheriting eternal life. When the lawyer was told that he should love his neighbor as himself, he asked, "And who is my neighbor?" Jesus answered him by telling the story of a traveling Samaritan who stopped at great cost to himself to aid a man who had been robbed by thieves. Others on that Jericho road where the incident had taken place passed by the man in distress without concern; they didn't want to get involved. But the Samaritan cared enough for a fellow human being's plight to stop and do something. Then Jesus asked the lawyer, "Who do you think was the neighbor?" This challenge the church can never lose without great peril to its mission. Those who compose the church fellowship are neighbors to everyone in need regardless of who they are.

Sometimes, however, Christians make the mistake of limiting the healing function of the church to caring for people in need, with little concern for changing the social and physical aspects of life that accompany and sometimes cause the need. Christians have a right and a responsibility to work, not only within the church, but also within their social and political allegiances to bring about justice for all people. Christianity does not fragment a person's life, giving him one set of standards for his life in the church and another set for his life in the world. As a matter of fact, the church gives no standards at all except the necessity to be a neighbor, to live in the world with faith active in love. Whatever the church can do to help men become whole and their society healthy is well worth the cost in time and effort.

Luther summed up this ministry of the church succinctly:

> . . . God is surpassingly rich in his grace: First, through the spoken word, by which the forgiveness of sin (the peculiar office of the Gospel) is preached to the whole world; second, through Baptism; third, through the holy Sacrament of the Altar; fourth, through the power of keys; and finally, through the mutual conversation and consolation of brethren.
>
> —*The Smalcald Articles, Part III, Article IV*

The pastor is chosen to lead a congregation in an effective ministry of nurture and service that makes the love of God meaningful to men where they are. Each member of that congregation is called by God to assist in that ministry in every way that he can, particularly through ministering to others at home, at work, and in every community of which he is a part.

Our Heavenly Father, Who dost surround our daily life with familiar things and well-known faces, and dost teach us to love our neighbor as ourself: We pray for all those among whom we live, our neighbors and acquaintances; for those with whom we work; for those whose lives ours will touch as we pass through the day's tasks and privileges; as well as for our dearest friends and near relations, humbly committing them all to Thy favor and care, beseeching Thee to guard and preserve them and us from all dangers of body and soul, that, by Thy grace and ever present help, we may so live now that we may dwell with Thee in the life that knows no ending; through Jesus Christ, our Lord. Amen.

—COLLECTS AND PRAYERS

8

THE CHURCH'S MINISTRY TO THE WORLD

ONE of the significant passages of the New Testament tells us:

> You are a chosen race, a royal priesthood, a holy nation,
> God's own people, that you may declare the wonderful
> deeds of him who called you out of darkness into his
> marvelous light. —*1 Peter 2:9*

These words describe the motivation for the Christian life.
The initiative is God's. That is the very heart of our Christian
commitment. As Christians and church members, we are
expected to participate personally in the functions of the
people of God. We follow God's will for our lives naturally
and gladly because we love him. We accept our vocation as
his people out of thankfulness, not in order to win God's favor.
"Good works" have an important place in the Christian life
but only as the normal results of a Christian's conduct. Although this distinction may seem academic, it is very important.

THE CHRISTIAN'S CALLING

We frequently use the phrase the Christian's calling, or the
Christian vocation, to refer to the personal invitation God
extends to each of us to belong to his people. The terms are
confusing to modern ears because we often think of a calling

as a direct summons to professional religious work, and a vocation as any particular line of work.

Popular usage has severely limited the term the Christian's calling. We are accustomed to speak of "calling a pastor" when a congregation seeks a leader. We often say that deaconesses or other people in full-time church work are following their calling. In both instances, we really mean that these people, pastor and lay people alike, are engaged in church occupations. Actually, a pastor or a deaconess has the very same Christian vocation that all Christians do. We are all called to witness and to serve in whatever occupations we happen to have. A pastor discharges his Christian vocation through his profession as a clergyman, and others discharge their vocations through their particular professions or jobs. There is no such thing, then, as a Christian businessman or a Christian doctor or a Christian secretary or a Christian housewife. There are only Christians who happen to be businessmen or doctors or secretaries or housewives. They fulfill their Christian vocation through their occupations. Our daily work situations usually provide strategic occasions, places, and opportunities for the exercise of our Christian calling. In addition, however, there are opportunities for the Christian's witness and service through every waking hour: in family experiences, in exercising citizenship responsibilities and privileges, in recreational activities, and in all the contacts he has with others.

Whenever we discuss the Christian's calling, it is important to remember that God takes the initiative; he is the one who calls. He calls men into fellowship with himself and with each other. Paul puts it this way:

We know that in everything God works for good with those who love him, who are called according to his purpose. For those whom he foreknew he also predestined to be conformed to the image of his Son, in order that he might be the firstborn among many brethren. And those

whom he predestined he also called; and those whom he
called he also justified; and those whom he justified he
also glorified.   —*Romans 8:28-30*

The fact that Paul mixes his reference to the call of God
with such matters as predestination, justification, and glorification shows that to his mind, at least, the Christian vocation
cannot be separated from the totality of God's dealings with
man. We can appreciate this by remembering how we feel
compelled to respond when someone goes out of his way to
do something helpful for us. Somehow we feel we must try
to repay the debt even though no repayment is really possible.
Our sense of obligation stems from our sense of gratitude.
Similarly, our acceptance of our Christian vocation stems from
our thankful attitude toward God.

The Christian's calling sounds very personal and individualistic. To a degree, it is—but it is really social in nature.
Did you notice the collective nouns in the quotation from
Peter's Letter? "A chosen race, a royal priesthood, a holy
nation, God's own people." God's personal call to each of you
is in terms of a strong, corporate relationship with the rest of
his people. In like manner, God's call requires our personal
response, but it suggests that we work together to fulfill his
purposes for his world. Reread 1 Corinthians 12:12-14, 26-27
for another insight into the same truth. Paul was conscious of
the interdependence among Christians in their God-oriented
community life. Each person brings his own gifts of the Holy
Spirit to the fellowship for the good of the whole.

GETTING ALONG TOGETHER

Not many of us would be inclined to dispute the Christian
contention that a spirit of harmony and mutual support should
prevail among Christians. But this ideal is not just for the
sake of getting along together and avoiding the unpleasantness
of conflict; the Bible sees such harmony as a natural fruit of
Christian faith and as an indispensable base of effective vocation. The First Letter of John expresses this truth:

Beloved, let us love one another; for love is of God, and
he who loves is born of God and knows God. He who
does not love does not know God; for God is love. In
this the love of God was made manifest among us, that
God sent his only Son into the world, so that we might
live through him. In this is love, not that we loved God
but that he loved us and sent his Son to be the expiation
for our sins. Beloved, if God so loved us, we also ought
to love one another. *—1 John 4:7-11*

Clearly, the New Testament recognizes the motivation for
Christian fellowship as being God's own love in operation
among men. At the same time, the New Testament brings this
lofty motivation down to earth and makes it the practical base
from which Christians can effectively carry out their calling.

This emphasis upon harmonious fellowship among Christians should not stand in the way of a genuine appreciation
for individual differences in interests, capabilities, and ways
of expressing the Christian calling. Paul, in particular, made
a great deal of this fact and tried to get Christians to accept
individual differences as an asset rather than a liability to
their community life in the Spirit. Within the limits required
to maintain harmonious fellowship, Christians are not only
free to express their individual gifts but are expected to do so.
If your special abilities are committed to God and handled
with true Christian concern for the good of the whole congregation, they add immeasurably to the strength of the church.
As a member of the church, you want a good working relationship with your fellow members—but not at the price of
blind conformity.

When it comes to witness and service, many church members make the mistake of thinking that they have to talk and
act as a pastor would talk and act in a similar situation. But
the gifts of the Holy Spirit to you and to your pastor are
probably quite different, and the circumstances in which you
express your calling are certainly very different. God expects
you to be yourself, to use your own gifts with imagination and

faithfulness. This is the best contribution you can make to the effectiveness of Christian ministry in your community.

THE UNIVERSAL PRIESTHOOD

The New Testament concept of the priesthood of believers is quite different from the meaning we usually associate with the priesthood. We usually think of a priest as a professional Christian leader who is given a special status by God to serve as a bridge between God and men. Yet the New Testament makes clear that all Christians have this special status, that they are priests of God, ordained by baptism to serve God and man.

As priests, we come to God directly in prayer and worship, we read and study his Word, we seek his guidance for living. Likewise as priests, we have a joyous obligation to serve him and our fellowmen in love. On one occasion, Jesus was asked which of all the commandments in the law he thought was greatest. Without hesitation, he quoted Deuteronomy 6:5 and Leviticus 19:18 from the Old Testament Scriptures:

> "You shall love the Lord your God with all your heart, and with all your soul, and with all your mind. This is the great and first commandment. And a second is like it, You shall love your neighbor as yourself. On these two commandments depend all the law and the prophets."
> —Matthew 22:37-40

Obviously, the first part of Jesus' famous summary of the law describes a duty that is simply beyond man's abilities. How can a man love God perfectly and fully? Nor can we fulfill the second part of the Great Commandment and really love our neighbors as ourselves, not matter how noble our intentions. Our priesthood, therefore, is always marked by our imperfections and our constant need of God's forgiveness. If we take our priesthood seriously, we must come to him daily for guidance in learning how to love. John points out that only as we receive God's love can we really practice love in return: "We love, because he first loved us" (1 John 4:19). To serve our neighbors wherever they are and with whatever service they need is to allow God's love to work through us. This happens right in the midst of everyday life—at home or along the roadside, at the factory or the office, on the beach or the golf course—wherever people need help. Where are we to find our neighbors but in the everyday world? That fact alone gives immeasurable significance to the ministry of the laity. People expect pastors to repeat the "party line." Often, they are more apt to listen when the man who works next to them speaks of serving God and lives as a Christian in their presence. They identify with someone who faces the same problems they face, who understands the pressures, temptations, and conflicts that confront them.

Christianity, of course, is no escape from the world but a way of living in the world contentedly and effectively. Whether we like it or not, we are involved in everyday life. Here are some areas of life in the world that offer special opportunities for lay ministry.

WORK AND WITNESS

It hardly comes as news that work is an important part of life. Work occupies a large share of your time and energy. It greatly influences the kind of home you have, the size of your family, the amount and type of recreation you enjoy, your social standing and the type and variety of organizations to which you belong, your political point of view, and, in general, your way of life and outlook. Perhaps nothing illustrates the crucial place of work in our lives as much as the plight of the unemployed who feel useless and unwanted. The place work occupies in our lives and our dependence upon it makes it a truly critical area for the exercise of priesthood.

Even the relatively good working conditions which prevail today hurt people physically, mentally, and spiritually. Industrial organizations have grown larger and more complex. The impersonality brought on by automation tends to produce working conditions in which workers find less and less sense of personal fulfillment. For many people, work has lost its meaning as a way of life. It has become a necessary drudgery to provide the income we need to do other things. It is hard to help someone feel his job is important when he is only one cog in a gigantic piece of production equipment, but we can help him feel that he is important because he belongs to God. It may be that the role of today's Christian is first of all to help others realize their calling to live as Christians in whatever line of work they perform. Second, we can strengthen them in their troubles and give them assurance that someone really cares what they do and what happens to them.

THE PRIEST AS CITIZEN

There are many people who feel strongly that religion and politics do not mix. This feeling comes in part from extending the traditional American separation between church and state to include separation of religion and politics. In a society containing many religious groups, separation between church and state is necessary to insure justice for all. Yet for a Christian, it is neither possible nor desirable for his political life and convictions to be divorced from his religious life and convictions. Part of the trouble comes from a misunderstanding of politics. Too many people identify political activity with a bitterly partisan spirit; they look on politicians as people frequently less than honorable in their campaign tactics and their conduct of office.

There may be good reasons for this inbred suspicion. Politics has much to do with acquiring and using power and therefore offers a lively set of temptations. Even for that reason alone, a Christian citizen should welcome the opportunity to bring Christian morality and ethics to bear upon the political scene.

However, if we are to realize the tremendous potential the political arena has for the practice of our priesthood, we need to remind ourselves what politics really means. In essence, politics is the process by which men work out arrangements for living together. No social group can endure for long without some sort of rules to regulate its behavior. All through history there have been such arrangements. The Ten Commandments, for instance, can be understood as a very basic political document through which God's covenant with his people could be put into practical effect as a basis for their life together.

Political activity affords a Christian constant opportunity to exert an influence on the side of public morality and justice. You will find a great deal of help for handling your political responsibilities in the Lutheran concept of the two realms of grace and law. Political arrangements belong to the realm of law. But this is still God's realm, the scene of his activity in history. The Christian simultaneously is a citizen of the kingdom of God and a citizen of his own country. He has, therefore, two sets of privileges and responsibilities. Jesus recognized the legitimate claims of the state on its citizens. He said, "Render therefore to Caesar the things that are Caesar's, and to God the things that are God's." (Matthew 22:21). However, he did not hesitate to challenge the power of the state when it was in conflict with the will of God. The political arena is a challenging field for a Christian's witness and service because there he can join his neighbors in establishing just laws to protect the rights of all people in the nation—Christians and non-Christians alike.

THE CHRISTIAN AT PLAY

Because of reduced work schedules or early retirement, many people are finding themselves with more time on their hands than they know how to use. If present trends continue, it seems inevitable that the standard workweek will be further reduced in the near future. It may soon be the case that for the first time in history, man will have more time to devote to recreation than he is required to devote to productive labor. This prospect is both promising and dangerous. It is promising because it can release an almost unbelievable amount of human energy to work for the creation of a better world for all people. It is dangerous because of our long tradition of viewing work as good and leisure activities as a questionable waste of time.

We need a strong sense of Christian vocation if we are to be able to appreciate the values and meanings in our leisure time. Rest and recreation are both necessary to equip us to perform our jobs effectively. It is wholesome to know how to relax and enjoy life. But beyond caring for our own needs and desires, leisure means opportunities for service. The needs of men are so many and so great that any amount of our freedom from work that we give toward meeting them is a valuable extension of our serving God.

Standing beside another human being and lending support and friendship as he works through the temptations and crises of his life is priesthood in action, particularly if your presence and friendship convey the presence and concern of Christ.

A HEALTHY BALANCE

To be effective priests of God, we need a healthy balance of worship and service. The Gospel writers note that in between Christ's acts of healing and teaching he frequently went to a quiet place for prayer. Then he would return to his tasks refreshed. We should follow his example in developing our regular routines. Like him, we need a healthy balance between our participation in the church fellowship and our witness on behalf of that fellowship.

There are always temptations to forget the needed balance. For instance, the more aware we become of God's grace and forgiveness, the more we want to spend our days as close to his healing presence as we can. There were times in the history of the church when men felt that they served God best by renouncing the world and living apart from it in isolation. Our modern equivalent of isolation can be in what we commonly call "church work"—that is, the housekeeping chores that pertain to the life of our congregation. This is certainly not to say that the housekeeping chores are unimportant, or that you should not assume a fair share of them for the good of your congregation—but the Christian life needs to be balanced.

We can easily become so busy caring for the congregation's needs that we lose sight of our responsibility to serve outside its walls. Naturally, we respond to God's grace by gathering regularly around the Word and sacraments to express grati-tude to God in public worship and to be renewed by forgive-ness and fellowship. These activities are essential to our spir-itual growth. However, if we limit the Christian life to these practices, we can become ingrown and self-centered. A healthy Christian life needs regular nourishment at the Lord's table and constant support in the faith by fellow Christians, but it also needs the satisfaction of spending itself in witness and service in the world. Think of this balance in your life as a Christian in terms of "coming" and "going," or "assembling" and "sent." The "nurture" side of congregational life exists in part to equip you with the necessary motivation and skill for your priesthood in the world, the "outreach" side of congre-gational life.

EVANGELISM AND SOCIAL MINISTRY

Evangelism is an expression of the church's concern for the spiritual well-being of all men. It seeks to help those who are not Christian become members of the body of believers. In this manner, the congregation feels it is obeying Christ's com-mission to "go and make disciples of all nations." Even if you are not taking an active part in your congregation's program of evangelism, you have the privilege of inviting others to join the people of God and share in God's gifts to that fellow-ship. Actually, you can't help being an evangelist so long as you are identified as a Christian. Your witness can either sup-port the cause of Christ or detract from it, but in either case you are a witness. Remember that Paul said Christians are ambassadors of Christ. An ambassador of Christ is obligated to represent his Lord with fidelity and effectiveness wherever he may be.

The social ministry program of the congregation goes hand in hand with evangelism. In fact, it is often difficult to distinguish between the two. But, in general, social ministry is a channel for the congregation's ministry of service. It is helping people in trouble or guiding them to find practical answers to their problems. Ignorance, disease, alcoholism, poverty—these still plague people. The church wants to help in any way it can. It may establish a marital counseling service, or provide food for the hungry. It may offer guided study hours for children in overcrowded slums, or establish clinics for medical help.

As in the case of evangelism, the congregation's program of social ministry, while offering many opportunities for service, should be regarded as a training ground for the exercise of Christian concern in the daily walks of life. When you are really alive to Christian concern, there is never a lack of opportunity to express it; the supply of "neighbors" in need is unlimited.

PUBLIC PRIESTHOOD

Take any average day and try to count the number of people you meet in every sort of transaction or simply pass by on your travels. Would you be surprised to learn that you probably saw more people in one day than Christ did in a year?

It is a physical impossibility to engage in a deep personal relationship with every person you encounter. But this doesn't mean that even our most casual and functional contacts have to be cold and unfriendly. They can be pleasant, helpful, and, above all, kindly. Many of our contacts involve little more than a simple transaction in which we perform a service for someone or they do so for us. If we are on the serving end, the least we can do is to perform our function cheerfully and well; and if we are on the receiving end, we can at least acknowledge the other as a person and accept his service gracefully and with gratitude.

There is also a way in which our priesthood can be exercised for persons we do not know. It is by our witness and service through the so-called public sectors of life. This includes politics at every level, organizations and movements, and every situation where a Christian can bring his faith to bear upon public life either directly or indirectly. One direct way of doing this is by the way we vote. What determines the way you cast your ballot? Would you be more likely to vote for a candidate who pledges to reduce taxes or one who pledges to serve humanity? It is possible that tax reduction and human welfare can go together in some instances, but most of us are realistic enough to realize that such a happy combination is unlikely. You can multiply the example by illustrations in education, housing, conservation, industry, transportation, communication, and international relationships. Our society is becoming so complex and the population so large that most public problems can only be solved by public means. More and more Christian individuals and congregations are going to face the necessity of extending their witness into public affairs.

A FULL CHRISTIAN LIFE

The full Christian life that we have been discussing is expressed simply by the writer of the Letter to the Ephesians:

> For by grace you have been saved through faith; and this is not your own doing, it is the gift of God. . . . For we are his workmanship, created in Christ Jesus for good works, which God prepared beforehand, that we should walk in them.   —*Ephesians 2:8-10*

Here again we note the strong connection between God's gift and our good works. It is like the relationship a river has with its source. The river carries the water from its beginning all the way to its eventual end. Only by flowing is the river a blessing to men; if it ceases to flow, it stagnates and in a sense dies.

Similarly, the Christian life flows from its source in the grace of God. Through nurture and outreach, the people of God keep their lives fresh and flowing out in their world. Whatever our abilities and interests, there is an important place for each of us in the vital fellowship of the people of God. For God has called us to be Christians and gives us all we need to live joyfully and trustingly in our world.

Another pertinent passage from the Letter to the Ephesians offers a summary of the vital purpose of Christianity for every one of us:

And his gifts were that some should be apostles, some prophets, some evangelists, some pastors and teachers, for the equipment of the saints, for the work of ministry, for building up the body of Christ, until we all attain to the unity of the faith and of the knowledge of the Son of God, to mature manhood, to the measure of the stature of the fulness of Christ; so that we may no longer be children, tossed to and fro and carried about with every wind of doctrine, by the cunning of men, by their crafti- ness in deceitful wiles. Rather, speaking the truth in love, we are to grow up in every way into him who is the head, into Christ, from whom the whole body, joined and knit together by every joint with which it is supplied, when each part is working properly, makes bodily growth and upbuilds itself in love. —Ephesians 4:11-16

We give thanks, O God, for all happiness we have known in past years; for all moments of loveliness and beauty; for work attempted and done; for all that has made our hearts grateful and lifted them to Thee. May we not for any present grief or weakness forget the gladness we have known, but keep our memories bright with praise and love. May we consider the lilies of the field and the birds of the air, as our Saviour Jesus said, and give thanks to Thee for the beauty in the world, O Heavenly Father, Source of love and light and life, through Him Whose grace is sufficient for us, and Whose strength is made perfect in weakness; even the same Jesus Christ our Lord. Amen.

—Author Unknown

PSALM 23

The Lord *is my shepherd, I shall not want;*
  he makes me lie down in green pastures.
He leads me beside still waters;
  he restores my soul.
He leads me in paths of righteousness
  For his name's sake.

Even though I walk through the valley of the shadow
    of death,
  I fear no evil;
for thou art with me;
  thy rod and thy staff,
  they comfort me.

Thou preparest a table before me
  in the presence of my enemies;
thou anointest my head with oil,
  my cup overflows.
Surely goodness and mercy shall follow me
  all the days of my life;
and I shall dwell in the house of the Lord *for ever.*
                              —Revised Standard Version

THE SMALL CATECHISM

BY MARTIN LUTHER
IN CONTEMPORARY ENGLISH

Luther's *Small Catechism* is essentially a handbook of basic Christian instruction for the family and the congregation. Luther was dismayed with the ignorance of the people in Saxony. He resolved to help them learn the Christian truths in a way that would be both accurate and meaningful. He prepared this Catechism in 1529 "in the plain form in which the head of the family should teach . . . his household" for home and church use.

PART ONE

ThE TEN COMMANDMENTS

I am the Lord your God.

The First Commandment

You shall have no other gods.

WHAT DOES THIS MEAN FOR US?

We are to fear, love, and trust God above anything else.

The Second Commandment

You shall not take the name of the Lord your God in vain.

WHAT DOES THIS MEAN FOR US?

We are to fear and love God so that we do not use his name to curse, swear, lie, or deceive, but call on him in prayer, praise, and thanksgiving.

The Third Commandment

Remember the Sabbath day, to keep it holy.

WHAT DOES THIS MEAN FOR US?

We are to fear and love God so that we do not neglect his Word and the preaching of it, but regard it as holy and gladly hear and learn it.

The Fourth Commandment

Honor your father and your mother.

WHAT DOES THIS MEAN FOR US?

We are to fear and love God so that we do not despise or anger our parents and others in authority, but respect, obey, love, and serve them.

THE FIFTH COMMANDMENT

You shall not kill.

WHAT DOES THIS MEAN FOR US?

We are to fear and love God so that we do not hurt our neighbor in any way, but help him in all his physical needs.

THE SIXTH COMMANDMENT

You shall not commit adultery.

WHAT DOES THIS MEAN FOR US?

We are to fear and love God so that in matters of sex our words and conduct are pure and honorable, and husband and wife love and respect each other.

THE SEVENTH COMMANDMENT

You shall not steal.

WHAT DOES THIS MEAN FOR US?

We are to fear and love God so that we do not take our neighbor's money or property, or get them in any dishonest way, but help him to improve and protect his property and means of making a living.

THE EIGHTH COMMANDMENT

You shall not bear false witness against your neighbor.

WHAT DOES THIS MEAN FOR US?

We are to fear and love God so that we do not betray, slander, or lie about our neighbor, but defend him, speak well of him, and explain his actions in the kindest way.

The Ninth Commandment

You shall not covet your neighbor's house.

WHAT DOES THIS MEAN FOR US?

We are to fear and love God so that we do not desire to get our neighbor's possessions by scheming, or by pretending to have a right to them, but always help him keep what is his.

The Tenth Commandment

You shall not covet your neighbor's wife, or his man-servant, or his maidservant, or his cattle, or anything that is your neighbor's.

WHAT DOES THIS MEAN FOR US?

We are to fear and love God so that we do not tempt or coax away from our neighbor his wife or his workers, but encourage them to remain loyal.

What does God say of all these commandments?

He says: "I, the Lord your God, am a jealous God, visiting the iniquity of the fathers upon the children to the third and fourth generation of those who hate me, but showing steadfast love to thousands of those who love me and keep my commandments."

WHAT DOES THIS MEAN FOR US?

God warns that he will punish all who break these commandments. Therefore we are to fear his wrath and not disobey him. But he promises grace and every blessing to all who keep these commandments. Therefore we are to love and trust him, and gladly do what he commands.

PART TWO

THE APOSTLES' CREED

THE FIRST ARTICLE

I believe in God the Father almighty, Maker of heaven and earth.

WHAT DOES THIS MEAN?

I believe that God has created me and all that exists. He has given me and still preserves my body and soul with all their powers.

He provides me with food and clothing, home and family, daily work, and all I need from day to day. God also protects me in time of danger and guards me from every evil.

All this he does out of fatherly and divine goodness and mercy, though I do not deserve it. Therefore I surely ought to thank and praise, serve and obey him. This is most certainly true.

THE SECOND ARTICLE

And in Jesus Christ his only Son, our Lord; who was conceived by the Holy Ghost, born of the Virgin Mary; suffered under Pontius Pilate, was crucified, dead, and buried; he descended into hell; the third day he rose again from the dead; he ascended into heaven, and sitteth on the right hand of God the Father almighty; from thence he shall come to judge the quick and the dead.

WHAT DOES THIS MEAN?

I believe that Jesus Christ—true God, Son of the Father from eternity, and true man, born of the Virgin Mary—is my Lord.

He has redeemed me, a lost and condemned person, saved me at great cost from sin, death, and the power of the devil—not with silver or gold, but with his holy and precious blood and his innocent suffering and death. All this he has done that I may be his own, live under him in his kingdom, and serve him in everlasting righteousness, innocence, and blessedness, just as he is risen from the dead and lives and rules eternally. This is most certainly true.

THE THIRD ARTICLE

I believe in the Holy Ghost; the holy Christian church, the communion of saints; the forgiveness of sins; the resurrection of the body; and the life everlasting. Amen.

WHAT DOES THIS MEAN?

I believe that I cannot by my own understanding or effort believe in Jesus Christ my Lord, or come to him. But the Holy Spirit has called me through the Gospel, enlightened me with his gifts, and sanctified and kept me in true faith. In the same way he calls, gathers, enlightens, and sanctifies the whole Christian church on earth, and keeps it united with Jesus Christ in the one true faith.

In this Christian church day after day he fully forgives my sins and the sins of all believers. On the last day he will raise me and all the dead and give me and all believers in Christ eternal life.

This is most certainly true.

PART THREE

The Lord's Prayer

THE INTRODUCTION
Our Father who art in heaven.

WHAT DOES THIS MEAN?
Here God encourages us to believe that he is truly our Father and we are his children. We therefore are to pray to him with complete confidence just as children speak to their loving father.

THE FIRST PETITION
Hallowed be thy name.

WHAT DOES THIS MEAN?
God's name certainly is holy in itself, but we ask in this prayer that we may keep it holy.

When does this happen?
God's name is hallowed whenever his Word is rightly taught and we as children of God live in harmony with it. Help us to do this, heavenly Father!
But anyone who teaches or lives contrary to the Word of God dishonors God's name among us. Keep us from doing this, heavenly Father!

THE SECOND PETITION
Thy kingdom come.

WHAT DOES THIS MEAN?
God's kingdom comes indeed without our praying for it, but we ask in this prayer that it may come also to us.

When does this happen?
God's kingdom comes when our heavenly Father gives us his Holy Spirit, so that by his grace we believe his holy Word and live a godly life on earth now and in heaven forever.

THE THIRD PETITION

Thy will be done on earth as it is in heaven.

WHAT DOES THIS MEAN?

The good and gracious will of God is surely done without our prayer, but we ask in this prayer that it may be done also among us.

When does this happen?

God's will is done when he hinders and defeats every evil scheme and purpose of the devil, the world, and our sinful self, which would prevent us from keeping his name holy and would oppose the coming of his kingdom. And his will is done when he strengthens our faith and keeps us firm in his Word as long as we live.

THE FOURTH PETITION

Give us this day our daily bread.

WHAT DOES THIS MEAN?

God gives daily bread, even without our prayer, to all people, though sinful, but we ask in this prayer that he will help us to realize this and to receive our daily bread with thanks.

What is meant by "daily bread"?

Daily bread includes everything needed for this life, such as food and clothing, home and property, work and income, a devoted family, an orderly community, good government, favorable weather, peace and health, a good name, and true friends and neighbors.

THE FIFTH PETITION

And forgive us our trespasses, as we forgive those who trespass against us.

WHAT DOES THIS MEAN?

We ask in this prayer that our Father in heaven would not hold our sins against us and because of them refuse to hear our prayer.

And we pray that he would give us everything by grace, for we sin every day and deserve nothing but punishment. So we on our part will heartily forgive and gladly do good to those who sin against us.

THE SIXTH PETITION

And lead us not into temptation.

WHAT DOES THIS MEAN?

God tempts no one to sin, but we ask in this prayer that God would watch over us so that the devil, the world, and our sinful self may not deceive us and draw us into unbelief, despair, and other great and shameful sins.

And we pray that even though we are so tempted we may still win the final victory.

THE SEVENTH PETITION

But deliver us from evil.

WHAT DOES THIS MEAN?

We ask in this inclusive prayer that our heavenly Father would save us from every evil to body and soul, and at our last hour would mercifully take us from the troubles of this world to himself in heaven.

THE DOXOLOGY

For thine is the kingdom and the power and the glory forever and ever. Amen.

WHAT DOES "AMEN" MEAN?

Amen means *Yes, it shall be so.* We say *Amen* because we are certain that such petitions are pleasing to our Father in heaven. For he himself has commanded us to pray in this way and has promised to hear us.

PART FOUR

ThE SACRAMENT OF bAPTISM

1

What is Baptism?

The Sacrament of Baptism is not water only, but it is water used together with God's Word and by his command.

What is this Word?

In Matthew 28 our Lord Jesus Christ says: "Go therefore and make disciples of all nations, baptizing them in the name of the Father and of the Son and of the Holy Spirit."

2

What benefits does God give in Baptism?

In Baptism God forgives sin, delivers from death and the devil, and gives everlasting salvation to all who believe what he has promised.

What is God's promise?

In Mark 16 our Lord Jesus Christ says: "He who believes and is baptized will be saved; but he who does not believe will be condemned."

3

How can water do such great things?

It is not water that does these things, but God's Word with the water and our trust in this Word. Water by itself is only water, but with this Word it is a life-giving water which by grace gives the new birth through the Holy Spirit.

St. Paul writes in Titus 3: "He saved us . . . in virtue of his own mercy, by the washing of regeneration and renewal in the Holy Spirit, which he poured

out upon us richly through Jesus Christ our Savior,
so that we might be justified by his grace and become heirs in hope of eternal life. The saying is sure."

4

What does Baptism mean for daily living?

It means that our sinful self, with all its evil deeds
and desires, should be drowned through daily repentance; and that day after day a new self should arise
to live with God in righteousness and purity forever.
St. Paul writes in Romans 6: "We were buried therefore with him by Baptism into death, so that as
Christ was raised from the dead by the glory of the
Father, we too might walk in newness of life."

PART FIVE
The SACRAMENT OF holy COMMUNION

1

What is Holy Communion?

It is the sacrament instituted by Christ himself, in which he gives us his body and blood in and with the bread and wine.

What are the Words of Institution?

Our Lord Jesus Christ, in the night in which he was betrayed, took bread; and when he had given thanks, he broke it and gave it to his disciples, saying, "Take, eat, this is my body, which is given for you; this do in remembrance of me." After the same manner also he took the cup after supper, and when he had given thanks, he gave it to them, saying, "Drink of it, all of you; this cup is the new testament in my blood, which is shed for you, and for many, for the remission of sins; this do, as often as you drink it, in remembrance of me."

2

What benefits do we receive from this sacrament?

The benefits of this sacrament are pointed out by the words, *given and shed for you for the remission of sins.* These words assure us that in the sacrament we receive forgiveness of sins, life, and salvation. For where there is forgiveness of sins, there is also life and salvation.

3

How can eating and drinking do all this?

It is not eating and drinking that does this, but the words, *given and shed for you for the remission of sins.* These words, along with eating and drinking, are the main thing in the sacrament. And whoever believes these words has exactly what they say, forgiveness of sins.

4

When is a person rightly prepared to receive this sacrament?

Fasting and other outward preparations serve a good purpose. However, that person is well prepared and worthy who believes these words, *given and shed for you for the remission of sins.* But anyone who does not believe these words, or doubts them, is neither prepared nor worthy, for the words *for you* require simply a believing heart.

The Office of the Keys

What is the "Office of the Keys"?

It is that authority which Christ gave to his church to forgive the sins of those who repent and to declare to those who do not repent that their sins are not forgiven.

What are the words of Christ?

Our Lord Jesus Christ said to his disciples: "Receive the Holy Spirit. If you forgive the sins of any, they are forgiven; if you retain the sins of any, they are retained." —John 20:23

"Truly, I say to you, whatever you bind on earth shall be bound in heaven, and whatever you loose on earth shall be loosed in heaven."—Matthew 18:18

Confession

What is private confession?

Private confession has two parts. First, we make a personal confession of sins to the pastor, and then we receive absolution, which means forgiveness as from God himself. This absolution we should not doubt, but firmly believe that thereby our sins are forgiven before God in heaven.

What sins should we confess?

Before God we should confess that we are guilty of all sins, even those which are not known to us, as we do in the Lord's Prayer. But in private confession, as before the pastor, we should confess only those sins which trouble us in heart and mind.

What are such sins?

We can examine our everyday life according to the Ten Commandments—for example, how we act toward father or mother, son or daughter, husband or wife, or toward the people with whom we work, and so on. We may ask ourselves whether we have been disobedient or unfaithful, bad-tempered or dishonest, or whether we have hurt anyone by word or deed.

How might we confess our sins privately?

We may say that we wish to confess our sins and to receive absolution in God's name. We may begin by saying, "I, a poor sinner, confess before God that I am guilty of many sins." Then we should name the sins that trouble us. We may close the confession with the words, "I repent of all these sins and pray for mercy. I promise to do better with God's help."

What if we are not troubled by any special sins?

We should not torture ourselves with imaginary sins. If we cannot think of any sins to confess (which would hardly ever happen), we need not name any in particular, but may receive absolution because we have already made a general confession to God.

How may we be assured of forgiveness?

The pastor may pronounce the absolution by saying, "By the authority of our Lord Jesus Christ I forgive you your sins in the name of the Father and of the Son and of the Holy Spirit. Amen."

Those who are heavily burdened in conscience the pastor may comfort and encourage with further assurances from God's Word.

LUTHER'S SEAL

Luther's prince, John Frederick, appointed Lazarus Spengler at Nuremberg to make a ring for Luther. Spengler sent Luther a preliminary sketch of the coat of arms, asking for Luther's approval. Luther wrote the following reply:

Grace and peace in Christ, Honored Dear Sir and Friend:

Since you wish to know whether they have got my seal right, I will tell you how I originally planned my coat-of-arms as a symbol of my theology.

The first thing should be a cross, black, on a heart retaining its natural color, to remind me that it is faith in the Crucified that saves us. A person can only become righteous when he believes with his whole heart. And though it be a black cross, mortifying the flesh and purposely inflicting pain, it does not change the color of the heart nor destroy its nature. It does not kill, but rather preserves life. For the just shall live by faith, namely, faith in the Crucified.

This heart should be set in the midst of a white rose, to show that such faith yields joy, peace and comfort such as the world cannot give. That is why the rose is white and not red, for white is the color of spirits and angels.

This rose is placed on a field of heavenly blue, because such spiritual joy and faith are a beginning of heavenly joys to come, which are even now possessed by faith and understood in hope, although they are not yet evident to the outward eye.

And, encircling this field is a ring of gold, to signify that this bliss of heaven endures forever, and is more precious than all earthly pleasures and possessions, even as gold is the most precious of metals.

May Christ our dear Lord be with your spirit until it attains to that life. Amen.

worship

In Christian worship God meets man in a personal relationship. In this two-way communication, God reveals himself as the loving Creator Father and calls us, through Christ, into a new life of fellowship and forgiveness. Our response in this divine-human encounter takes such forms as adoration and praise, confession of our sin, thanksgiving for God's gifts, attention to God's Word, prayer for ourselves and others, and the dedication of our lives in joyful service.

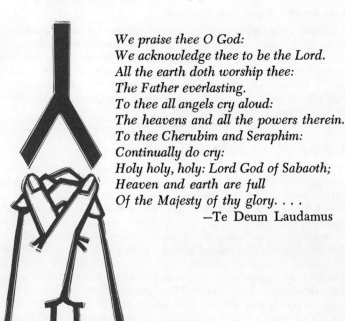

We praise thee O God:
We acknowledge thee to be the Lord.
All the earth doth worship thee:
The Father everlasting.
To thee all angels cry aloud:
The heavens and all the powers therein.
To thee Cherubim and Seraphim:
Continually do cry:
Holy holy, holy: Lord God of Sabaoth;
Heaven and earth are full
Of the Majesty of thy glory. . . .
                    —Te Deum Laudamus

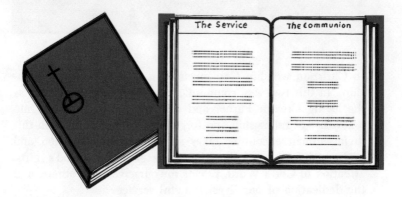

The Service Book and Hymnal

In 1958 eight Lutheran denominations collaborated in the publication of the *Service Book and Hymnal*. Since then mergers have reduced the eight denominations to two which represent two-thirds of American Lutheranism. The *Service Book and Hymnal* is actually two volumes in one: a service book offering basic resources for the public worship of God and a hymnal containing a comprehensive and ecumenical collection of 602 hymns.

The Service and Its Musical Settings

"The Service" is the name given to the chief order of corporate worship in the Lutheran church. The text of The Service appears on pages 1-14 of the *Service Book and Hymnal*. Three musical settings are provided for it. The First Setting (*SBH*, pp. 15-40) is based largely upon Anglican chant sung in speech rhythm. In this style of chanting or singing, the time value of the music follows the natural rhythm of the spoken word. The Second Setting (*SBH*, pp. 41-70) is based upon the chorale traditions of German and Scandinavian Lutheran usage. The Third Setting (published in a separate booklet) is based upon plainsong, the earliest music of the church. Many congregations have learned more than one setting and alternate from one to the other during seasons of the church year in order to provide greater variety in their worship. The three musical settings are illustrative of the richness of the musical traditions which have flowed into the present usage of the Lutheran church in Canada and in the United States.

The SERVICE

Parts	Explanation	Posture
The Invocation	We call upon the Name of the Holy Trinity. Matt. 18:20; Col. 3:17	Stand

THE PREPARATION

Parts	Explanation	Posture
The Confession of Sins and Absolution	We prepare our hearts and are assured that God forgives us. Heb. 10:22; James 5:16	Stand or Kneel

I. THE OFFICE OF THE WORD

Parts	Explanation	Posture
The Introit for the Day	The entrance hymn which sets the keynote for the Day. Psalms 100:4	Stand
The Gloria Patri	Rom. 16:27; Eph. 3:21 Phil. 4:20; Rev. 1:6	Stand
The Kyrie	We express our need and our concern for others. Luke 17:13; 18:13, 38, 39 Heb. 4:16	Stand
The Gloria in Excelsis	Confident that God supplies our need, we adore the Lord God. Luke 2:14	Stand
The Salutation and Response *	Minister and people greet one another and prepare to attend to the important matters which follow. Ruth 2:14; Luke 1:28; 2 Thess. 3:16; 2 Tim. 4:22	Stand
The Collect for the Day	A brief prayer for the family of God. Phil. 4:6	Stand or Kneel

* Adapted from "Encounter and Response" (an outline of the Liturgy or The Service of Holy Communion from the Service Book and Hymnal of the Lutheran Church in America, prepared by the Department of Worship).

Parts	Explanation	Posture
The Lesson (Old Testament)	God speaks through the words of those who waited for the Messiah in Israel.	Sit
The Epistle for the Day	God speaks through the apostles, special messengers of the Lord.	Sit
The Gradual for the Day or for the Season (or the Alleluia or the Lenten Sentence)	A hymn which looks back upon the Epistle and forward with joy to the Gospel.	Sit
The Gospel for the Day (with responses before and after)	God speaks to us through the words and life of his Son Jesus Christ.	Stand
The Apostles' Creed (The Nicene Creed)	We profess our belief in the mighty acts of God. Mk. 16:16; John 20:28-29; Acts 8:36-37; Acts 2:42	Stand
The Hymn	This is the chief hymn of the day and stresses the church's observance.	Stand
The Sermon	The minister unfolds to us the truth of God's Word. 1 Cor. 1:23	Sit
	The sermon concludes with the blessing of God's peace which overrides all doubts (Phil. 4:7) to which we respond "Amen."	Stand

II. THE OFFICE OF THE SACRAMENT

The Offering, The Offertory (the preparation of the bread and wine)	In response to God who has spoken to us we offer Him our gifts . . . money and bread and wine . . . as symbols of the offering of ourselves. We also offer our possessions, our time, our abilities, as instruments of his will. Eph. 5:2; Mark 12:33; Matt. 5:23-24; Rom. 12:1	Stand

Parts	Explanation	Posture
The Prayer of the Church	We offer our common supplications with the whole church of Christ. 1 Tim. 2:1-5	*Stand or Kneel*
The Preface (with the Proper Prefaces)	Our response of Thanksgiving (Ps. 26:6, 7) is joined by the church in all times and in all places as we sing—	*Stand*
The Sanctus	—"Holy, Holy, Holy" Isaiah 6:1-4; Rev. 4:8; Matt. 21:8-9	*Stand*
The Prayer of Thanksgiving	Our Thanksgiving or eucharist is for God's love in Christ who through bread and wine gives us his body and blood— Luke 22:8-20; 1 Cor. 11:23-29; 1 Cor. 10:16	*Stand or Kneel*
The Lord's Prayer	—and our thanks are summed up in our Lord's own words— Matt. 6:9-13; Luke 11:2-4	*Stand or Kneel*
The Pax	—through whom we know peace. John 20:19-21	*Stand or Kneel*
The Agnus Dei	Preparing to be made one with Him. We adore the Lamb of God, seeking his mercy and peace. John 1:29; Isaiah 53	*Stand*
The Communion	We receive the body and blood of Christ and are made one with God to the forgiveness of sins, life, and salvation. John 6:53-56	*Go to the altar and receive Holy Communion*
The Post Communion The Nunc Dimittis The Prayer The Salutation The Benedicamus	We give thanks to God and pray that he will lead us to wider and continued service in the world. Matt. 26:30; Luke 2:29-32	*Stand*
The Benediction	The minister dismisses us in the name of God and sends us forth to do His will. Numbers 6:24-26	*Stand*

ORDERS OF WORSHIP

In addition to The Service, the *Service Book and Hymnal* provides guidance for using other orders of worship such as:

Matins

Matins (*SBH*, p. 129) is a service of praise and prayer for use at the beginning of the day.

Vespers

Vespers (*SBH*, p. 141) is more contemplative in mood than Matins, though similar in structure. Vespers is an ideal order of thanksgiving and prayer for use toward the end of the day.

The Litany

The Litany (*SBH*, p. 156) is one of the oldest and finest prayers of the church. It may be used as part of other orders of worship or as a special office by itself on days of penitence and prayer. The Litany covers the full range of human reliance on the mercy and goodness of God.

The Suffrages

The Suffrages ("prayers of intercession") are poetic forms of prayer. The General Suffrages (*SBH*, p. 153), The Morning Suffrages (*SBH*, p. 154), and The Evening Suffrages (*SBH*, p. 155) are three flexible forms of worship designed for use when a brief service of worship is desired. The Suffrages can also be used as part of other services and in devotions.

The *Service Book and Hymnal* contains a number of additional worship resources for use in corporate worship or private devotions such as:

The Psalms (*SBH*, p. 162)—a representative collection of the most helpful poems, arranged for responsive reading.

The Canticles (*SBH*, p. 215)—other worship poetry from the Bible arranged for responsive reading.

Collects and Prayers (*SBH*, p. 218)—a collection of brief prayers arranged topically for easy reference.

ThE OCCASIONAL SERVICES

Significant events of life are occasions for meaningful worship. The church has wisely provided worship forms for these events. The following orders, although quite functional, are worshipful in mood and corporate in scope, stressing the reality of the people of God by incorporating personal and family events into the worship life of the congregation.

Baptism

Baptism (*SBH*, p. 242) is a sacramental service celebrating the incorporation of a new Christian into the life of the people of God. Slightly different orders are provided for adults and infants, but in each case the chief emphasis is upon God's act.

Confirmation

Confirmation (*SBH*, p. 245) is a rite in which a baptized Christian, after appropriate instruction, is admitted to the privileges and responsibilities of church membership on a more mature level.

Public Confession

Public Confession is intended primarily as a service of preparation for Holy Communion. The Order for Public Confession has two forms, a brief form or use with The Service (*SBH*, p. 247) and a longer form for a special preparatory service (*SBH*, p. 249).

Burial

Burial is one of the most beautiful of the church's orders. The Order for the Burial of the Dead (*SBH*, p. 253) enshrines the death of a Christian in the faith and hope of the church and ministers to the bereaved in an atmosphere of quiet confidence and trust.

Marriage

Marriage (*SBH*, p. 270) asks the blessing of God upon the marriage and brings to marriage a clear witness to the support of the congregation and of the church.

The Occasional Service Book, a companion to the *Service Book and Hymnal*, contains the services listed here as well as a wide selection of other orders and offices for special occasions and events.

ḣymnoḋy

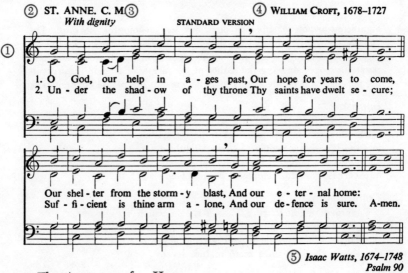

② ST. ANNE. C. M③   ④ WILLIAM CROFT, 1678–1727
With dignity   STANDARD VERSION

1. O God, our help in a - ges past, Our hope for years to come,
2. Un - der the shad - ow of thy throne Thy saints have dwelt se - cure;

Our shel - ter from the storm - y blast, And our e - ter - nal home:
Suf - fi - cient is thine arm a - lone, And our de - fence is sure. A-men.

⑤ *Isaac Watts, 1674–1748*
Psalm 90

The Anatomy of a Hymn

① *Top line* of music, the melody or soprano line. The other parts, in descending order, are: alto, tenor, and bass. Some hymns are marked for unison singing.

② *Name of tune.* Most hymns have names for convenient identification.

③ *The meter* (number of syllables per line). Abbreviations are often used such as: C. M. (common meter—8 6, 8 6), S. M. (short meter —6 6, 8 6), L. M. (long meter—8 8, 8 8), C. M. D. (common meter doubled), S. M. D. (short meter doubled).

④ *Composer* of the tune with dates of his birth and death. The arranger of a tune may also be listed.

⑤ *Author* of the text with dates of his birth and death. A translator may be listed.

What Is a Hymn?

All of the fine arts may enrich the worship of the church. Music, however, occupies a place of special significance as a companion of worship. In liturgy and hymnody, music is a versatile and valuable vehicle of worship. A hymn unites music with a poetic text for singing. In this merger of art forms, music serves to exalt and enhance the message of the text. Music also creates a mood, shapes attitudes, and encourages action. Congregations are seldom more united in thought, in spirit, and in act than when singing a hymn.

The *Service Book and Hymnal* offers an ecumenical collection of Christian hymns which span virtually the whole history of Christianity and represent contributions from many denominational sources.

> *The birth of Jesus was announced in song, and the last act of worship of our Lord and his Disciples was the singing of a hymn. Sacred song, rooted in the Hebrew tradition, occupied from the first a pre-eminent position in Christian worship. The earliest hymns were psalms and canticles. Initially the people sang them, though by the fourth century in the East, and by the seventh in the West, they had become part of the liturgy and a matter for the clergy and the choirs. Not again until the time of the Reformation was the hymn restored to the people as their rightful heritage in worship.*
> —Introduction to the Common Hymnal

the church year

The Church Year is a calendar of special days and seasons which Christians have followed for centuries. It offers an annual pattern for proclaiming and teaching the central truths of Christianity. Each Sunday bears a title related to the Church Year.

> *Advent Season,* with its four Sundays of preparation for Christmas, looks forward to the coming of Christ.
>
> *Christmas,* December 25, celebrates the birth of Christ.
>
> *Epiphany Season* tells the good news of Christ to the world for four to six Sundays depending on Easter's date.
>
> *Pre-Lenten Season* has three Sundays with names that tell how long it is to Easter: Septuagesima (70 days), Sexagesima (60 days), and Quinquagesima (50 days).
>
> *Lenten Season* is a time of repentance and preparation for Easter. The first day is Ash Wednesday. There are six Sundays. The sixth is known as Palm Sunday, which introduces Holy Week. Maundy Thursday, the commemoration of the Last Supper, and Good Friday, the day of the Crucifixion, are part of this week.
>
> *Easter* is always the first Sunday after the first full moon of spring, and celebrates Christ's resurrection. Five Sundays after Easter celebrate the joy of the event. Forty days after Easter, on a Thursday, is Ascension Day.
>
> *Pentecost,* fifty days after Easter, is the church's birthday.
>
> *Trinity Season* begins on the Sunday after Pentecost. It uses from 22 to 27 Sundays, depending on the date of Easter, to emphasize teachings about faith and life.

The Propers of The Service

Certain parts of The Service such as the Introit, the Collect, the Lesson, the Epistle, the Gradual, and the Gospel always reflect a specific theme of the Church Year. These parts are called the Propers. Each Sunday and special day has its own set (*SBH,* p. 75).

The Lectionary

Published in either the Revised Standard Version or the King James Version, the Lectionary offers the complete texts of the Lessons, Epistles, and Gospels for the Church Year. The Lectionary is a companion to the *Service Book and Hymnal.*

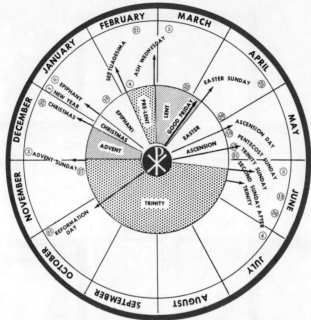

Note: The fixed dates of the Church Year are printed in straight lines, e.g., Christmas, December 25. The movable dates of the Church Year are indicated by curved printing, e.g., Easter may occur on any date between March 22 and April 25.

Liturgical Colors

Each season of the Church Year has a symbolic color:

White (Christmas, Epiphany, Easter), purity and holiness of God

Purple (Advent, Lent), Jesus' humiliation and suffering for us

Green (Pre-Lent, Trinity), the color of nature, Christian growth

Red (Pentecost, Reformation Sunday, special festivals), blood of martyrs and fire of the Spirit

Black (Good Friday), sadness and mourning

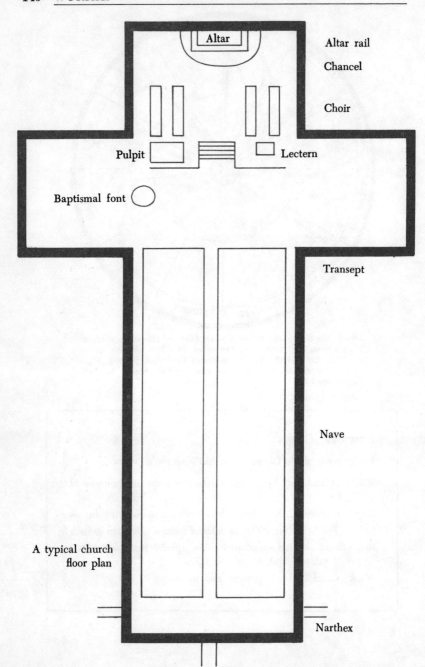

Altar

Altar rail

Chancel

Choir

Pulpit   Lectern

Baptismal font

Transept

Nave

A typical church
floor plan

Narthex

Chalice

Paten

Ciborium

Acolyte

Flagon

Stole

Surplice

Cassock

The *altar* is usually furnished with a cross (or crucifix), candles, flowers, and a missal stand to hold the Service Book. To these are added the sacramental vessels when they are to be used.

Paraments are cloth hangings used on the altar, pulpit, and lectern. Together with the pastor's stole, they are always the liturgical color of the current Church Year season. Altar hangings are called frontals; pulpit and lectern hangings are called antependia.

SYMBOLS

 The Holy Trinity

 God the Father

 The Holy Trinity

 Christ, Christianity

 The fish: Christ

 Greek letters for Christ, first and last

Greek letters for Christ

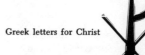

Greek letters for Jesus

Thorncrown: Christ

Lamb of God: Christ

The dove: God the Holy Spirit

Eternal life

The church

Christian hope

Symbols, the sign language of the church, convey ideas, concepts, and images to the mind. Some of the more common symbols are on these pages.

Holy Communion

Holy Baptism

Peace

The Word of God

The four Gospels

PRAYER

Prayer is the natural expression of your Christian life. It arises out of the confluence of your trust in God and the awareness of your own needs. Prayer comes naturally to the Christian and both nourishes and expresses his faith.

The Elements of Prayer

Adoration is the essential mood of prayer. It is praising God because he *is*.

Confession is the act of telling God we are sorry for our sin, of seeking his forgiveness.

Thanksgiving is the chief reason for prayer and in most instances its main theme. It includes gratitude for God's grace, concern, and gifts, and may be quite pointed and specific in its frame of reference.

Petition is expression of honestly felt personal needs in conscious and humble expectation that they will be met with God's blessing.

Intercession is the wider dimension of prayer in which the needs of others are presented to God.

Your Personal Devotional Life

As a Christian, you need special quiet moments during the day when you can be alone with God, talk with him, and listen to his word of guidance.

Personal devotions usually include the reading of Scripture, meditation, and prayer. But around this minimal base you can develop a meaningful, daily conversation with God. Regularity and concentration are the keys to effective periods of personal devotions.

ChE BIBLE

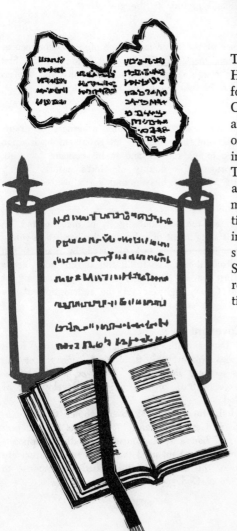

This church acknowledges the Holy Scriptures as the norm for the faith and life of the Church. The Holy Scriptures are the divinely inspired record of God's redemptive act in Christ, for which the Old Testament prepared the way and which the New Testament proclaims. In the continuation of this proclamation in the Church, God still speaks through the Holy Scriptures and realizes His redemptive purpose generation after generation.

—Article II, Section 3,
LCA Constitution

The Olo Testament

The Old Testament recounts the mighty acts of God in choosing and working with a special people. The thirty-nine books represent several types of literature and cover thousands of years of experience. The Old Testament is background and prelude to the gospel.

Creation

One of the great themes of the Bible is the complete dependence of all creation, including man, on God. This insight begins in the first pages of Genesis, where through stories of timeless beauty and ageless truth, creation is anchored in the loving purpose of God.

The Nature of God

The Old Testament preserves and protects the "otherness" or transcendence of God. At the same time, there is an equal emphasis upon God's "nearness" expressed in his activity and in his concern for man. The Apostles' Creed expresses the duality of God's nature, ". . . God the Father almighty, Maker of heaven and earth."

The Nature of Man

The Old Testament stresses the potential dignity of man created "in the image of God" and his assignment of subduing the earth and ruling it. However, this image is defaced, the task distorted, by man's selfish pretensions and willful disobedience. To fulfill this destiny man needs help. Almost from its first pages, the Bible foresees the coming of this help in the form of God's mightiest act—the redemption of the world in Jesus Christ.

Abraham and the Covenant

The Old Testament begins with a broad, almost cosmic focus intended to announce and support the theological concepts of the Hebrews. The emphasis narrows significantly, however, at the beginning of Genesis 12, to concentrate on the religious development of Israel, the people of God.

Abraham is considered the father of the chosen people. God's covenant with him, described in Genesis 15 and 17, accounts for the profound conviction that Israel had a special mission by divine appointment. At a later time, the apostle Paul used the covenantal relationship as the perfect prototype of the Christian faith: obedient response to the free promise and grace of God.

Moses and the Law

The Book of Exodus contains the key to the Old Testament. Recounting as it does the deliverance of the Hebrew people from bondage in Egypt, it assumes a position in the Old Testament similar to the accounts of the crucifixion and resurrection of Christ in the New Testament. For the Jews, the deliverance is the great watershed experience of their history, which marked the faith of the covenant community.

The sequel to deliverance is the giving of the Law. The Law described boundaries for human attitudes and conduct, to protect and support the covenant community. Because Moses figured so prominently in both the Exodus and the codification of the Law, he emerges as the central human hero of the Old Testament.

David and the Kingdom

Next to Moses, no one in Hebrew history looms larger than the victorious warrior, King David. He was the type of leader who inspires legends and makes it difficult to separate fact from fiction. Yet David was a very human personality, a genius at war and politics, but probably not as wise a ruler as tradition has insisted. However, David exemplifies the glorious era when the Hebrew nation reached its zenith and spawned the spiritual decline that eventually led to national oblivion.

The Prophets and the Word of God

The Old Testament makes little if any distinction between God's acting and speaking. Yet he chose men to be prophets, to be his special spokesmen, to present his Word to his people. The Hebrew prophets who carried on their ministry between 800 and 400 B.C. form a galaxy of spiritual magnitude. Isaiah, Jeremiah, Amos, and Hosea, among others, and their messages, are truly immortal. They were the interpreters of Israel's decline, the challengers of Israel's concern. Most of the Old Testament as we know it today is almost certainly the product of an attempted reformation spurred by prophetic voices around 600 B.C.

Poetry and Praise

For the Hebrews, regular worship of God occupied the central place in their religious lives. Many parts of the Old Testament preserve their literature, a magnificent gift to human desire for exalted language to use in worship and praise. The Psalms alone constitute a major contribution to the world's worship language. They directly influenced the liturgical expressions of the Christian church. Wisdom literature such as Proverbs, the sheer poetry of Second Isaiah, the drama of Job enrich the spiritual insights of the Old Testament.

The books of the old testament

The Books of the Law

These five books form a preface to the history of the people of God and introduce most of the fundamental theological concepts.

Genesis, the book of beginnings, asserts the dependence of all creation upon God and lays the foundation for the unique sense of vocation of the people of God.

Exodus tells of God's freeing the Hebrews from slavery in Egypt, his giving of the Law to Moses, his establishing a covenantal relationship with his people. Exodus 20 reports the Ten Commandments which Moses received on Mount Sinai.

Leviticus reports the origins of cultic life and the evolution of the priesthood, prominent features of Israel's worship.

Numbers recounts a national census and details the ordering of the Hebrews' theocracy.

Deuteronomy, associated with religious reform and renewal late in the Old Testament period, sounds this theme: Return to the simple faith and sturdy virtues of your fathers and all will be well.

The Books of History

In the Promised Land the Israelite nation made its place in the world and then began its descent into historical oblivion. These books contain the most reliable history and proclaim in the Bible that God controls history.

Joshua describes the settlement of the Hebrews in the Promised Land. Their military leader, Joshua, personifies their struggle for homeland and national purpose.

Judges relates the events of a turbulent period when judges ruled the people of Israel, a loose confederation of tribes. This book is notable for its consistent linking of national fulfillment and obedient faith in God.

Ruth is a romantic interlude which conveys a message of tolerance and respect for other nations.

1 and 2 Samuel record the events which mark Israel's coming of age as a significant world power. Facing Philistine "aggression," the Hebrew tribes became a nation under leaders such as Samuel, Saul, and David.

1 and 2 Kings describe the decline and fall of the Hebrew nation from the splendor of Solomon through the tragedy of civil war which divided the country into two nations to the collapse of the Southern Kingdom, Judah.

1 and 2 Chronicles, written later than *Kings,* review the reigns of David and Solomon and detail the Southern Kingdom's history. Both *Kings* and *Chronicles* close after the fall of Jerusalem and the people's deportation into Babylonian exile.

Ezra and *Nehemiah* deal with the Hebrews returning from captivity in Babylon to restore their homeland. The books reflect the Hebrews' intense attachment to the Law, which began in exile and sustained them during the extremely difficult years of rebuilding and restoration.

Esther is the story of the Jewish queen of a Persian ruler. She worked arduously on behalf of her people.

The Books of Poetry and Wisdom

The literature of devotion and reflection reveals the Hebrews' character more accurately than do their histories.

Job is basically a drama dealing with the deepest questions of life, calamity, bereavement, and physical suffering which confront people and test their faith. *Job* probes the depths of the human predicament.

Psalms is the hymnbook of the Hebrew nation, a collection of poems reflecting man's relationship with God. *Psalms* offers a wide variety of worship resources.

Proverbs expresses practical advice for daily living in short pithy sayings.

Ecclesiastes, written with heavy skepticism toward man's pretensions, insists that life must be weighed against the inevitable fact of death.

Song of Solomon, frankly sensual in its glorification of human love, is probably a collection of songs used at weddings.

The Major Prophets

This section contains longer prophetic books as well as Lamentations and Daniel.

Isaiah, seeing an Assyrian invasion threat, gave his nation hope through repentance and reformation. Key ideas are the coming Messiah and the faithful remnant. Chapter 40–66 are the work of another man in the period of Babylonian exile.

Jeremiah, speaking from Judah during the Exile, proclaims: God prefers righteousness of life over faithfulness in ceremonial observances. The prophet teaches the need of a new covenant written on the heart.

Lamentations consists of five lyric poems mourning the fall of Jerusalem and seeking meaning in calamity. *Lamentations* was written by the prophet Jeremiah.

Ezekiel, writing from captivity in Babylon, stresses the transcendence of God over the events of history. He uses vivid symbolism to convey his message.

Daniel is apocalyptic literature using past history written in the future tense, visions and vivid imagery, and a famous person (Daniel) to convey a message of strength for the people of God under persecution.

The Minor Prophets

These books are labeled "minor" because of their brevity.

Hosea, writing during the final days of the Northern Kingdom, uses an unhappy family situation to demonstrate God's patient forgiveness and restoration of unfaithful Israel.

Joel, a native of Jerusalem, broadens the Jewish concept of God by proclaiming God's judgment over all nations.

Amos, a herdsman from Tekoa, announces with righteous wrath the judgment of God on the sinful people as well as on their enemies.

Obadiah is a vindictive message against Edom to enforce the prophetic belief that evil cannot ultimately prevail.

Jonah is a sermon on the necessity of man's duty to aid in God's work.

Micah champions pure worship, God's promise of forgiveness, hope in the nation's restoration.

Nahum's cry for justice has appeal for all oppressed people.

Habakkuk stresses God's eventual punishment of the wicked and that "the righteous shall live by his faith" (2:4).

Zephaniah preaches against corrupt practices and religious perversions of both Israel and her enemies, promises comfort to those who serve the Lord.

Haggai seeks to renew the Hebrews' sense of national purpose after the return from exile.

Zechariah offers a series of visions and oracles to purify the nation, picturing the Messiah as a good shepherd, a man of peace.

Malachi emphasizes faithfulness to the Lord's covenant and its teachings. He points to the Lord's coming messenger as preparation for a day of judgment, and God's fatherly concern for all.

OLD TESTAMENT IN HISTORY

ATE B.C.	WORLD HISTORY	HEBREW HISTORY	PERSONALITIES		WRITINGS
2000	Egyptian Empire Babylonian Empire Hammurabi	Migration to Palestine Sojourn in Egypt	Abraham Isaac Jacob Joseph		
1500 1300	Trojan War Rameses II	The Exodus Conquest of	Moses Joshua	Deborah	Oral traditions:
1100		Canaan Judges	Samuel		Miriam's song Noah's blessing
1000		The kingdom	Saul		Creation stories
	Homer's *Iliad* and *Odyssey*	Civil war Division of kingdom:	David Solomon		
		Judah Samaria		Omri Ahab	
750			Elijah Elisha		
	Assyrian Empire	Fall of Samaria (722)	Hezekiah	Manasseh Josiah	Amos, Hosea, Isaiah, Micah, Kings, Zephaniah, Nahum, Samuel, Habakkuk, Job,
620 600	Buddha Confucius Babylonian conquest	King Josiah's reform Fall of Jerusalem (586)		Zedekiah	Jeremiah, Lamentations, Joshua, Judges, Ezekiel, 2 Isaiah, Haggai, Zechariah
500	Cryus the Great	Return from exile (538)			
	Persian Empire Greek-Persian wars	Jerusalem and Temple rebuilt	Ezra	Nehemiah	Obadiah, Ruth, Jonah Joel, Song of Solomon Malachi
	Age of Pericles Socrates Plato Aristotle				Ezra, Nehemiah Proverbs, Chronicles Esther Genesis, Exodus, Leviticus, Numbers, Deuteronomy (Final edition) Ecclesiastes Daniel
350	Alexander the Great (332) Greek Empire Roman Empire	Alexander conquers Palestine Seleucid kings Maccabean revolt	Judas Maccabeus		
150	Han Dynasty Julius Caesar	Roman rule Herod the Great	Birth of Christ		Apocryphal Old Testament books Dead Sea Scrolls

ThE NEW TESTAMENT

Jesus Christ

The New Testament begins with four Gospels which tell the story of Christ's life and teachings.

Born in Bethlehem about A.D. 6, Jesus spent a normal childhood and youth in and around Nazareth. In early manhood, following his baptism by John the Baptist, he began a ministry which was to last not more than three or four years. But he would have an impact upon the world greater than that of any other person in history.

His ministry began within the framework of his ancestral religion, but after his rejection by the Hebrew leaders, he concentrated upon training a band of twelve disciples to expand and continue his ministry. He was crucified about A.D. 29 as an agitator and possible rebel against Rome.

However, after three days in the tomb, he appeared among the disciples and others, and continued his

instructions for some forty days. Then he disappeared again. The disciples were utterly convinced that God had raised him from the dead, fulfilling the promises God made in the Scriptures. On this basis, they proclaimed Christ the expected Messiah and began a mission of preaching his gospel to the ends of the earth. They were convinced that Jesus Christ was the living Son of God who could reconcile all men with God.

The Teachings of Christ

It was said of Jesus that he taught with unique authority. This means that he taught with confident assurance as he presented new insights about God and his will for men. He frequently used parables and pithy sayings to encapsulate the truth. In content, his teachings combined the ancient law with the moral insights of the prophets and adapted them with peculiar clarity to everyday life on the basis of love. His consistent themes were that the kingdom of God had invaded life, that God was a loving, forgiving heavenly Father for all who would accept him, that men were to live as "salt," as "light," as disciples. He promised men the presence of God the Holy Spirit to guide and strengthen them in his absence.

The Christian Church

Shortly after Jesus returned to God the Father, a Christian community was formed on Pentecost under the Spirit's power. It began under the leadership of the apostles and at first assumed a communal form. However, its rapid expansion made this an impractical arrangement as the church had to adapt to life in the world around it sufficiently to begin the process of conquering the world for Christ. The early church was characterized by its absolute faith that it was the instrument of the Holy Spirit to complete the mission which Christ had begun of winning all men to God.

The Work of Paul

Originally a bitter enemy of the Christian religion, Paul was converted around A.D. 34 and became the missionary supreme of the new faith. His four personal journeys extended the church in Asia Minor and in Europe. His extensive correspondence gave systematic and relevant form to the faith. His letters formed the New Testament's core.

Letters and Visions

In addition to the four Gospels and the letters of Paul, the New Testament also contains several letters attributed to various authors and the Book of Revelation, which is the New Testament's most extensive example of apocalyptic literature.

The books of the New Testament

The Gospels

Matthew presents the sayings and actions of Jesus in alternating rhythm. Probably the production of the church of Jerusalem, its flavor is distinctly Jewish-Christian. The Sermon on the Mount is in Chapters 5, 6, and 7.

Mark was the first Gospel written and served as a source for *Matthew* and *Luke*. *Mark* describes Jesus for Gentile readers as the powerful Son of God. The Gospel traditionally is associated with the church at Rome.

Luke, a traveling companion of Paul, writes of Jesus with lyric language. He presents Christ as the compassionate healer for all mankind. The familiar Christmas story is in Chapter 2.

John came later than the other Gospels and offers theological interpretation of the life and work of Christ. The Gospel represents a profound adaptation of the gospel to the prevailing Greek culture of the first century. *John* 3:16 is the gospel in miniature.

A Book of History

Acts, the work of Luke, tells the history of the church from Pentecost through some of its most exciting adventures. He describes the ministry of the apostles and Paul's missionary journeys.

Letters to Young Congregations

Romans is Paul's massive attempt to systematize Christian theology for the Christians in the church at Rome. Romans 12 is a guide to Christian living.

1 and 2 Corinthians are fragments of what were originally four letters. The first of the letters is a practical counterpart to Romans, dealing with thorny problems in the clear light of Christianity.

1 Corinthians 13 is a profound discussion of love. The second letter offers good insights into Paul's character and motivations.

Galatians, a letter of Paul's written to the churches in Galatia, is often referred to as the Magna Charta of man's evangelical freedom. Paul strongly insists that a man becomes right with God through his faith in Christ.

Ephesians, written to the church at Ephesus, deals with God's purpose in establishing and completing the church for both Jews and Gentiles. Ephesians describes the church as the living body of Christ.

Philippians, addressed to the church of Philippi, is among the most beautiful of Paul's letters. It contains a memorable encouragement for all men to have the mind of Christ (2:5-11).

Colossians was written to the church at Colossae to correct their faulty thinking about Christ. False teachers taught errors. Paul emphasizes sufficiency of Christ alone and suggests a Christian ethic guided by love.

1 Thessalonians is Paul's instruction of new converts to guide them in Christian conduct and their understanding of Christ's second coming.

2 Thessalonians contains Paul's additional thoughts about the second coming. He rebukes idleness and encourages responsible daily work.

Letters to Pastors

1 Timothy provides guidance in ordering worship and dealing with church administration.

2 Timothy encourages faith and endurance in preaching the gospel and in living by it.

Titus describes responsibilities of elders, ways of dealing with varying groups in the church, and ethical living.

Letters to New Christians

Philemon deals with the problem of a runaway slave and throws some valuable light on the Christian attitude toward man.

Hebrews is intended to convince Jews that Christianity, logically as well as historically, stems from the Old Testament Scripture.

James is a sermon reminding Christians how to live; their faith must lead to good works.

1 Peter gives encouragement and hope to Christians in times of danger and persecution.

2 Peter strengthens faith in Christ's second coming and warns against false teachers.

1 John stresses the love of God and the love of one's fellowman. He points out that "perfect love casts out fear" (4:18).

2 John is a brief discourse on love as the law of life.

3 John encourages imitating good rather than evil.

Jude warns against false teachers corrupting the church.

An Apocalyptic Vision

Revelation uses poetic images to encourage Christians facing trials and troubles to remain faithful. In a series of vivid visions, John the Seer powerfully affirms God's victory over all the world's evil.

pALESTINE IN JESUS' DAY

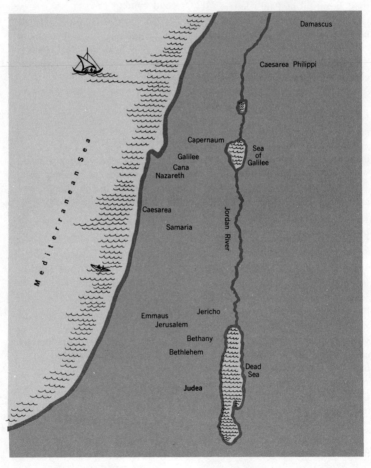

NEW TESTAMENT IN HISTORY

Date	World History	History of Christianity	Personalities	Writings
B.C. 6	Caesar Augustus, Roman emperor	Jesus born in Bethlehem	Herod the Great	
A.D. 10	Tiberius			
20		John baptizes / Jesus' ministry	John the Baptist / Jesus	
27		Jesus crucified / Jesus risen	The 12 Disciples	
30	Caligula	Church's birth / Stephen stoned	Peter / Stephen	Preaching of the apostles / Oral gospel
40	Claudius / Expulsion of Jews from Rome	Paul's conversion / Paul's missionary journeys	Paul / Philip	1 and 2 Thessalonians
50	Nero	Jerusalem Council / Paul at Corinth	Luke	Corinthians / Galatians / Romans / Colossians
60		Paul reaches Rome		Philemon / Philippians
	Persecutions under Nero	Deaths of Peter and Paul	John (Bishop of Ephesus)	Philippians
70	Jewish Revolt / Jerusalem sacked by Titus' legions			Mark / James / Hebrews
80	Pompei destroyed by volcano		Matthew	Ephesians
	Domitian		Josephus / Luke-Acts	1 Peter
90				Revelation
100	Trajan	Persecution under Pliny	Clement of Rome / John	Epistles of John / Titus
110		Ignatius of Antioch martyred at Rome	Polycarp	2 Peter / Jude,
120	Hadrian			1 and 2 Timothy

CANONIZATION

The Bible represents a long process of determining which books should be included in its collection. The word canon means "rule," a measure for deciding the worthiness of the books as a norm for faith and life.

The Old Testament Canon

Although the first five books of the Bible were accepted as scripture about 400 B.C., the rest of the Old Testament was not officially recognized until c. A.D. 90. A council of rabbis at Jamnia formally agreed on the present thirty-nine books.

The Canon of the New Testament

An Easter letter written by Bishop Athanasius of Alexandria in 367 recommended that the church accept the present books of the New Testament. This official word was preceded by two hundred years of discussion and investigation in which the twenty-seven books now in the New Testament were considered many times.

Apocryphal Books

In 1546 the Roman Catholic Council of Trent acclaimed fifteen additional books as canonical. These books, which Protestants call the Apocrypha ("hidden"), include such writings as: Ecclesiasticus, 1 and 2 Maccabees, Tobit, Judith, 1 and 2 Esdras, The Wisdom of Solomon, Susanna, and Baruch. The books, which are printed in some Bibles, have a great deal of value because they reveal the religious thinking of the Jews between the two Testaments.

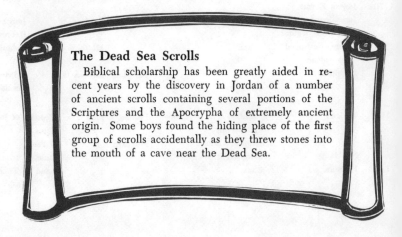

The Dead Sea Scrolls

Biblical scholarship has been greatly aided in recent years by the discovery in Jordan of a number of ancient scrolls containing several portions of the Scriptures and the Apocrypha of extremely ancient origin. Some boys found the hiding place of the first group of scrolls accidentally as they threw stones into the mouth of a cave near the Dead Sea.

TRANSLATIONS

The Vulgate

Translated into Latin by Jerome in A.D. 404, the Vulgate ("popular") version became the official version of the Western church for centuries. The Douay version is an English translation of the Vulgate.

Tyndale's Version

Tyndale translated the New Testament into English in 1525 and was working on the Old Testament when he was put to death as a heretic. His work has influenced English language versions ever since.

Luther's German Bible

Completed in 1534, Luther's translation into German was both scholarly and meaningful to life.

King James Version

Completed in 1611, this third authorized version is the most familiar in the English-speaking world.

American Standard Version

Completed in 1901, this was intended to update the King James Version, but never won popular acceptance.

Revised Standard Version

Published as the full Bible in 1952, the Revised Standard Version is basically a revision of the American Standard Version of 1901. The Revised Standard Version revisers sought to produce an accurate translation while retaining much of the beauty of the King James Version.

Phillips' Translation

In 1958, J. B. Phillips, an English scholar, produced a very readable New Testament translation characterized by paraphrasing and flowing vernacular English.

New English Bible

The New English Bible is a new translation representing the best of recent biblical scholarship and the best usages of modern English. The New Testament was published in 1961.

READING THE BIBLE

Above all, the Bible was designed to be read. Generally, it is not a recommended practice to read it from cover to cover, since the Bible does not flow in chronological order from Genesis to Revelation, but, like a library, tends to group its material into sections, each of which has some internal cohesion.

Read with Variety

Plan your reading to keep varied your study of biblical treasures. For instance, read a Gospel, then one of Paul's letters such as Philippians, perhaps an Old Testament book such as Genesis or Exodus, then another Gospel. Read brief selections from collections such as Psalms and Proverbs along with your regular reading. Develop your own method of reading that is most meaningful for your life.

Read by Ideas

One of the most profitable ways of reading the Bible is by pursuing an idea. To do this, you require the help of a Bible dictionary or a concordance which lists biblical words alphabetically and where they may be located. Use one of the more modern versions for the sake of clarity.

Read Prayerfully

Christians believe that God speaks in a special way through the Scriptures. A prayerful attitude when reading the Bible enables one to hear what God is saying.

Read Regularly

Regular reading of the Scriptures is also profitable. A regular visit with the Bible will establish an acquaintanceship which will make the Scriptures a familiar and trusted friend.

church history

"The past is prologue" to the present and the future of the church. The past is a major factor in determining what the church is at present, and its influence reaches into the future. It is impossible to understand the present or to prepare for the future unless we study the past. But history, in the biblical sense, is not only the past but also the present and the future, in all of which God is working toward the accomplishment of his own transcendent purposes.

The Incarnation is an event in history; it is the event in the light of which history can be understood as the work of God. The doctrine of the ascension is the church's way of confessing its belief that not only was Christ a part of history, but that he is now and will continue to be until history comes to its consummation in him. History is *his story*.

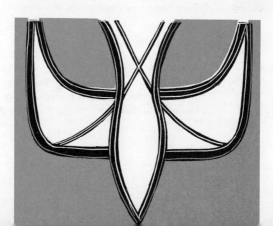

A TIME OF PLANTING

Pentecost

Fifty days after the resurrection of Christ, on Pentecost, the disciples and other believers were possessed by the Holy Spirit. They emerged from hiding and, under the leadership of men like Peter, began to proclaim the crucified and risen Jesus as the promised Savior of the world. Moreover, they said, his living Spirit was active, then and there, confronting men with the judgment and mercy of God. The time had come for men to turn in repentance and faith to receive the gift of life in the new age. Many believed, and thus the church began.

Paul

Saul, a zealous Jew, was converted by an experience on the Damascus road when on his way to harass Christians. He became Paul, the great missionary and theologian of the early church. His four journeys indelibly influenced Christian history. His many letters comprise half of the New Testament.

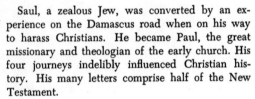

Ignatius

Bishop of Antioch, Ignatius (c. 50-109), is said to have been a pupil of the apostle John. He is believed to have been the first to refer to the church as "catholic." He is chiefly known today for fifteen "epistles" he wrote to fellow Christians before being martyred in Rome.

Polycarp

A disciple of the apostle John and a friend of Ignatius, Polycarp (c. 69-155), was Bishop of Smyrna. The last connecting link between the original apostles and the second-century church, Polycarp was sentenced to death at the stake.

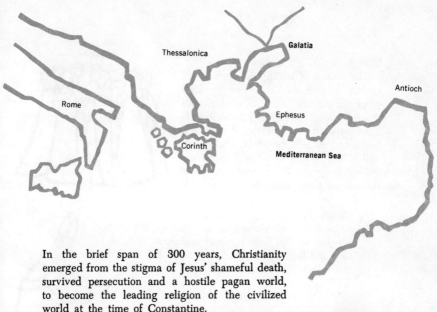

In the brief span of 300 years, Christianity emerged from the stigma of Jesus' shameful death, survived persecution and a hostile pagan world, to become the leading religion of the civilized world at the time of Constantine.

Justin Martyr

Justin Martyr (c. 100-165), a philosopher in the tradition of Plato, was converted to Christianity in early manhood and became a decisive leader of the second-century church. Before he was martyred by beheading, Justin enriched Christian thought with his writings, "Apologies" and "Dialogues."

Clement of Alexandria

Clement (c. 150-220), a great scholar and Christian, headed a catechetical school at Alexandria. Clement is chiefly remembered as the author of our oldest Christian hymn, "Shepherd of Tender Youth" (*SBH* 179).

A TIME OF MISSION

The Council of Nicaea

The council of leading theologians and church leaders was convened by Emperor Constantine, A.D. 325, to deal with the Arian controversy. The council reaffirmed the doctrine of the Trinity and renounced Arius's denial of Christ's divinity. The Nicene Creed in common use today, however, dates from the later Council of Constantinople, A.D. 381.

Athanasius

As Bishop of Alexandria, Athanasius (298-373) was one of the most vigorous opponents of heresies, and a staunch defender of the faith. One of the church's creeds is named in his honor.

Chrysostom

John Chrysostom (345-407) was one of the most famous preachers of the early church. He was appointed Archbishop of Constantinople in 397, but was deposed and exiled in 404.

Ambrose

Bishop Ambrose of Milan (340-397) was responsible for the conversion and baptism of Augustine. He originated the Ambrosian Chant and was a great church leader in the days when controversies split the church badly.

Augustine

Bishop Augustine of Hippo (354-430) was one of the church's great thinkers. His writings, such as *The City of God* and the *Confessions,* have profoundly influenced the church.

Patrick
(c. 389-461)
converted
Ireland.

Columba
(521-597)
led a mission
to Scotland.

King Olaf I
(c. 969-1000)
made Norway
Christian.

Augustine
(? -604)
worked in
England.

Vladimir I
(956-1015)
made Russia a
Greek Orthodox
country.

Ansgar
(801-865)
took the faith to
Denmark and
Sweden.

Boniface
(680?-755)
was apostle to the
Germans.

Charlemagne
(742-814)
made the Holy
Roman Empire
Christian.

King Clovis
(c. 466-511)
turned his Franks
Christian.

Missionaries and Converted Rulers Introduced Christianity to Europe.

Gregory the Great

Pope Gregory I (540-604) was the first monk to become pope. Gregory brought monasticism to the church's service, established the power of Rome in temporal affairs, and developed a strong system of ecclesiastical law.

A TIME OF TURMOIL

The sixteenth century broke upon a world that seemed to be coming apart at the seams. Feudalism was giving way to capitalism, the Renaissance preferred classical antiquity to medieval scholasticism, the Holy Roman Empire was teetering because of resurgent nationalism, Islam was rampant, and the New World was beginning to cast its lure.

Islam

Mohammed (c. 570-629), an Arabian, had visions of a new religion, Islam, based on the Old Testament. It was militant, conquering the Holy Land, North Africa, and Spain.

The Crusades

During the eleventh, twelfth, and thirteenth centuries, European Christians organized eight military expeditions to recover the Holy Land from Islam. No crusade was completely successful; most were failures. Historians now regard the social and economic effects of the Crusades of greater importance than any religious purpose they may have served.

Francis of Assisi

Founder of the Franciscan Order, Francis (1182-1226) taught a simple life of poverty, charity, and preaching the gospel. His *Little Flowers* is a devotional classic.

Richard the Lion-Hearted

King of England, Richard (1157-1199) became the central figure in the third crusade. The crusade, begun in 1189, succeeded in capturing Acre, but failed to take Jerusalem and restore the tomb of Christ to Christian possession.

Bernard of Clairvaux

Operating out of his monastery at Clairvaux, France, Bernard (1090-1153) became one of the most influential religious leaders in central Europe. He wrote many hymns and mystical devotional pieces, and was one of the moving spirits of the second crusade.

John Wycliffe

An English pastor, Wycliffe (c. 1329-1384) preached against the sins of his times. He organized college graduates into teams of traveling preachers and translated the Bible into English.

John Huss

In Prague, Bohemia, Huss (c. 1369-1415) preached against immoralities and tried to reform the church. He met a martyr's death.

Girolamo Savonarola

An Italian reformer and famous preacher, Savonarola (1452-1498) tried to bring about a moral and spiritual revival in Florence, Italy. He was burned as a heretic.

Thomas à Kempis

In the Netherlands, the Brethren of the Common Life urged service and devotion. Thomas (1380-1471) expressed their thought in his famous *Imitation of Christ*.

LUTHER AND THE REFORMATION

Luther, son of a German miner, studied law and then entered an Augustinian monastery to become a priest. Deeply religious, he became interested in studying and teaching the Bible. He was amazed by the differences between God's Word and church practices.

The Reformation begins

By the sixteenth century the church was in deep trouble. Corrupt officials and misguided religious practices abused the gospel. Ignorance and superstition combined to distort truth and confuse people. To Martin Luther (1483-1546), a professor at the University of Wittenberg, fell the task of working for reform.

Unscrupulous methods of raising money for church projects touched off the Reformation. On October 31, 1517, on the parish church door at Wittenberg, Luther nailed ninety-five theses or propositions for debating these and other troubling issues. Soon he was recognized as the leader of a sweeping reform movement. His stormy career was profoundly productive, as he taught, preached, wrote books on theology, hymns, and letters of counsel, and translated the Bible into German.

The Diet of Worms

Luther was summoned to appear before Emperor Charles V and high officials of the German empire on April 17 and 18, 1521. He refused to deny his writings or to change his teachings. He was branded a heretic and an outlaw; his books were ordered burned.

Philip Melanchthon

Luther's close associate, Melanchthon (1497-1560), authored the *Augsburg Confession* and its *Apology*.

The Augsburg Confession

The *Augsburg Confession,* a statement of belief, was presented by the German rulers who supported Luther to Emperor Charles V at Augsburg, June 25, 1530. This statement is the basis upon which political freedom was granted German Protestantism, and became the foundation for all of the confessional literature of the new Lutheran church.

THE BOOK OF CONCORD, 1580

This book, a collection of Lutheran teachings, contains:

The *Small Catechism* by Martin Luther (1529).
The *Large Catechism* by Martin Luther (1529).
The *Augsburg Confession* (1530).
The *Apology of the Augsburg Confession* (1531).
The *Smalcald Articles* (1537).
The *Formula of Concord* (1577).

The Spreading Reformation

John Calvin

A French lawyer, Calvin (1509-1564) had to flee his country because of his criticism of the church. In Switzerland, he became a pastor. He established a theocracy to make Geneva the "Rome of Protestantism." Though the project failed, Calvin became the leader of the reformed branch of Protestantism. His theological writings, *Institutes,* are famous for their system of Christian thought.

Ulrich Zwingli

Zwingli (1484-1531) was deeply influenced by Luther, and introduced reformation principles to Switzerland. He disagreed with Luther over the Lord's Supper and thereafter led his own branch of Protestantism.

Thomas Cranmer

Cranmer (1489-1556), the first Protestant Archbishop of Canterbury and the leader of the English Reformation, helped Henry VIII make the Church of England independent of Rome. Cranmer is regarded as the principal author of the Anglican statement of faith, the Thirty-Nine Articles. He was burned at the stake when Mary Tudor, a Catholic, came to the throne.

John Knox

Knox (c. 1505-1572), a Scottish reformer, spent some years in Geneva in exile during Catholic persecution. He became a disciple of Calvin, returning home in 1559 to openly challenge Rome. He won Scotland to his form of Calvinism (the Presbyterian church).

The Baptists

Held together by strong views on adult baptism by immersion, many different groups call themselves Baptists. Some trace their origin to the Anabaptist movement during the Reformation period, but their specific history began with John Smyth in Amsterdam in 1609. Strongly congregational in polity and individualistic in temperament, the Baptists have been among the first in the fight for political freedom.

The Counter-Reformation

Finally a movement of reform began within the Roman Catholic church at the height of the Reformation. Many conscientious leaders realized that much of the criticism of the church was justified. The Council of Trent (1562-63) called for founding of new religious orders, new definitions of doctrine, and minor internal changes. Ignatius Loyola (1495-1556) was the founder of the missionary-minded Jesuit Order and one of the strong leaders in the Counter-Reformation.

INTO ThE PRESENT

August Francke

Francke (1663-1727) was a German leader in the Pietist movement. Pietism was an attempt to balance intellectual understanding of Christianity with consecrated Christian living. Francke transformed the city of Halle into an influential spiritual center for a vast educational, welfare, and missionary enterprise.

Hans Hauge

Hauge (1771-1824), a Norwegian pietist and revivalist, inaugurated a voluntary lay activity which has had a continuing influence in Norway and in some American Lutheran circles.

Nikolai Grundtvig

Grundtvig (1783-1872), a Danish clergyman, combated intellectualism in his land by stressing emotional elements and the joy of Christianity. He wrote over 1400 hymns. The Grundtvig church in Copenhagen is shaped like a great pipe organ.

John Wesley

After a conversion experience, Wesley (1703-1791), an Anglican clergyman, and his brother Charles joined George Whitefield in a spiritual revival that swept through England and overflowed into America and Scotland. Although he never left the Church of England, Wesley laid the groundwork for the Methodist church.

Soren Kierkegaard

Kierkegaard (1813-1855), a Danish philosopher, is widely regarded as the father of existentialism. His emphasis upon religion as a life of decision has deeply influenced modern theology.

Robert Raikes

Raikes (1735-1811), and English publisher and philanthropist, began the Sunday school movement by employing women to teach children to read and to recite the Catechism. He lived to see Sunday schools established throughout England.

Nathan Söderblom

Söderblom (1866-1931), Archbishop of Uppsala, Sweden, spent a great part of his mature life working to bring about organized cooperation between churches, particularly on social questions, without securing doctrinal agreement. He was a leader in the 1925 "Life and Work" Conference at Stockholm that led to the formation of the World Council of Churches in 1948.

The Vatican Council

Called in 1962 by Pope John XXIII, the Second Vatican Council addressed itself to finding ways of translating Roman Catholic church theology and practices for the twentieth century.

LUTHERANS IN NORTH AMERICA

Dutch Lutherans in New York

Dutch Lutherans were among the first settlers in New Amsterdam (1623, Albany; 1625, Manhattan Island). Repressive policies of the Dutch West India Company, opposition from Dutch Reformed pastors, and the antagonism of Governor Stuyvesant made their lot extremely difficult. With New Amsterdam's surrender to the English in 1664, opposition ceased.

Swedish Lutherans in Delaware

Swedish Lutherans settled on the Delaware River in 1638. The colony grew until there were six or more congregations. The first Lutheran church building in America was erected under the leadership of Pastor John Campanius on Tinicum Island in 1646.

Justus Falckner

Falckner (1672-1723) was the first Lutheran minister ordained in America (November 24, 1703). He served a parish stretching from Long Island to Albany, New York.

Henry Melchior Muhlenberg

Muhlenberg (1711-1787) is justly called the "Patriarch of the Lutheran Church of America." His labors, organizational ability, and respect for the Confessions established the Lutheran church on American soil and developed a semicongregational polity for church government which neatly adapted the church to the American environment.

Canada

Lutherans entered Nova Scotia with the earliest English settlers and have continued immigration until the present day. Their distribution by national origin roughly parallels that of the United States, and for the most part their life has been linked with American churches. At present there is a strong sentiment among the 250,000 Canadian Lutherans for a church of their own.

The Norwegians

Vast numbers of Norwegian immigrants began to reach the Midwest in the 1830's. In 1846, under the leadership of men like Elling Eielsen (1804-83), they organized the Evangelical Lutheran Church of North America. Later others added small synods. Today the descendents of these Norwegian pioneers are part of the present American Lutheran Church.

The Danes

Danish immigrants, although present in considerable numbers, were less successful in establishing a flourishing church. Neither the Danish Lutheran Church in America, begun in 1872, nor the United Danish Lutheran Church in America, established in 1896, ever succeeded in gathering large numbers of their fellow countrymen into their folds.

The Swedes

By the 1840's Swedes were coming into the Midwest in great numbers. Stoutly adhering to confessionalism, and guided by men like Lars Paul Esbjörn (1808-63), they established the Augustana Lutheran Church in 1860. This vigorous group became a part of the Lutheran Church in America.

OTHER LUTHERAN CHURCHES

The Lutheran Church—Missouri Synod

Doctrinal conservatism and aggressive missionary zeal are characteristics of this large 2,700,000-member Lutheran church. Begun in 1847 among Lutheran immigrants from Saxony, the Missouri Synod was estab-

lished around St. Louis. During its early years the synod grew strong under the guidance of C. F. W. Walther, one of American Lutheranism's outstanding leaders. Recent decades have brought about an increasing willingness of Missouri to cooperate with other Lutherans in joint efforts as well as with other Christians.

The American Lutheran Church

On January 1, 1961, a merger between the Evangelical Lutheran Church, the American Lutheran Church, and the United Evangelical Lutheran Church gave birth to a new church, The American Lutheran Church. With its 2,600,000 members, it is an active partner with the Lutheran Church —Missouri Synod and the Lutheran Church in America, in the new cooperative Lutheran council. One of the ALC's outstanding leaders was J. A. A. Grabau.

Smaller Lutheran Bodies in North America
Apostolic Lutheran Church of America
Association of Free Lutheran Congregations
Church of the Lutheran Brethren of America
Church of the Lutheran Confession
Eielsen Synod
Evangelical Lutheran Synod
Synod of Evangelical Lutheran Churches
Wisconsin Evangelical Lutheran Synod

LUTHERAN CHURCH IN AMERICA

Remembering the prayer of our Lord Jesus Christ that His disciples might be one as He and the Father are one, and believing that His Spirit is ever leading His people toward unity in the household of God, we of the American Evangelical Lutheran Church, the Augustana Evangelical Lutheran Church, The Finnish Evangelical Lutheran Church of America, and The United Lutheran Church in America, persuaded that the time has come when His unifying power should be manifested through a united profession of faith by these churches and through forms of fellowship which will make for a more effective stewardship of His gifts to us, adopt this constitution to govern our common life in Him and our united witness to Him, praying that He who is the Lord of the Church may thereby lead us toward a more inclusive union of all Lutherans on this continent.

*—Preamble of the
LCA Constitution, 1962*

The STRUCTURE of The church

President: Dr. Franklin Clark Fry

From 1944 to 1962, Dr. Fry served as president of the United Lutheran Church in America. He has also been president of the Lutheran World Federation. He is chairman of the Central Committee and the Executive Committee of the World Council of Churches, president of the Lutheran World Relief, and a prominent figure in the National Council of Churches.

Secretary: Dr. Malvin H. Lundeen

From 1959 to 1962, Dr. Lundeen served as president of the Augustana Lutheran Church. He was the chairman of the Joint Committee on Lutheran Unity, which shaped the Lutheran Church in America.

The Treasurer: Carl M. Anderson

A layman and corporation executive, Mr. Anderson is active in both church and community affairs, and is currently on the boards of the LCA Common Investing Fund, the United Negro College Fund, the LCA Board of Publication, and Union Junior College, and is a trustee of Upsala College.

The Church in Convention

The ruling body of the LCA is the church in convention. The convention, composed of approximately 700 delegates elected by constituent synods, meets biennially. In broad terms, the convention reviews the work of the officers, the executive council, the boards, and the commissions, and determines both policy and program. The convention is representative democracy in action, assuring ultimate control of the church by congregations.

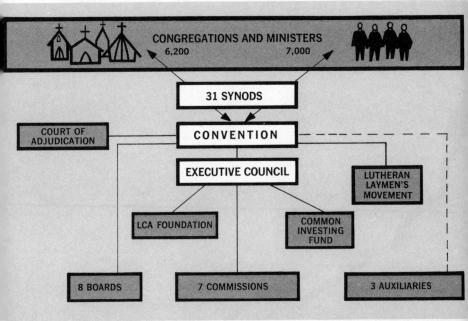

The Executive Council

Elected by the convention, the Executive Council is composed of thirty-three members: fifteen laymen, fifteen ministers, and the general officers of the church. The Executive Council acts for the church with broad authority to keep the church functioning smoothly between conventions. Its powers include: trusteeship, long-range planning, control of salaries, supervision of commissions, call of ministerial officers, and the general overseeing of ecumenical relationships.

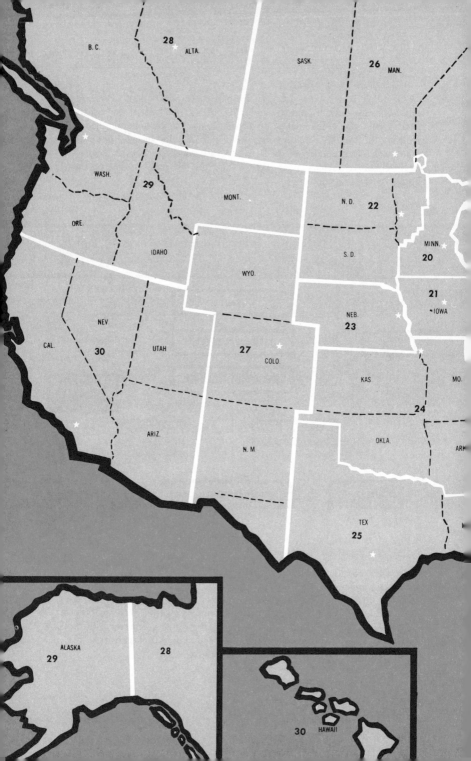

SYNOD	★ HEADQUARTERS
1. NEW ENGLAND	BOSTON
2. NEW YORK	NEW YORK
3. NEW JERSEY	TRENTON
4. EASTERN PENNSYLVANIA	PHILADELPHIA
5. CENTRAL PENNSYLVANIA	HARRISBURG
6. WESTERN PENNSYLVANIA	PITTSBURGH
7. MARYLAND	BALTIMORE
8. VIRGINIA	ROANOKE
9. NORTH CAROLINA	SALISBURY
10. SOUTH CAROLINA	COLUMBIA
11. SOUTHEASTERN	ATLANTA
12. FLORIDA	TAMPA
13. CARIBBEAN	BAYAMON, PUERTO RICO
14. OHIO	COLUMBUS
15. MICHIGAN	DETROIT
16. INDIANA-KENTUCKY	INDIANAPOLIS
17. EASTERN CANADA	KITCHENER, ONTARIO
18. WISCONSIN-UPPER MICHIGAN	MILWAUKEE
19. ILLINOIS	CHICAGO
20. MINNESOTA	MINNEAPOLIS
21. IOWA	DES MOINES
22. RED RIVER VALLEY	MOORHEAD, MINNESOTA
23. NEBRASKA	OMAHA
24. CENTRAL STATES	KANSAS CITY, MISSOURI
25. TEXAS-LOUISIANA	AUSTIN
26. CENTRAL CANADA	WINNIPEG
27. ROCKY MOUNTAIN	DENVER
28. WESTERN CANADA	EDMONTON
29. PACIFIC NORTHWEST	SEATTLE
30. PACIFIC SOUTHWEST	LOS ANGELES
31. SLOVAK-ZION (NON-GEOGRAPHICAL)	PITTSBURGH

The boards of the church

Eight boards constitute the major administrative units of the Lutheran Church in America and are assigned vital areas of responsibility. The convention elects twenty-one members to each board.

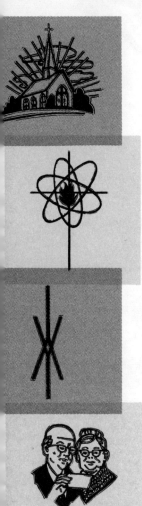

Board of American Missions

Wherever and whenever new congregations come to life, the Board of American Missions is in evidence, planning, planting, and servicing. Each year about 100 new missions are added to the number of young congregations given helpful guidance and financial assistance. Older congregations, especially those in urban and rural situations who have encountered special problems, are also helped.

Board of College Education, Church Vocations

In guiding an important part of the mission of the church, the board assists the synods in supporting twenty-five institutions of higher education. It seeks to implement church vocations by recruiting and placing qualified persons. Its responsibility in the area of deaconess work is closely related to the needs of the deaconess movement with its emphasis on training women for full-time work in the church.

Board of Parish Education

This board is responsible for developing a comprehensive program of Christian education for children, youth, and adults in local congregations. A broad new curriculum was introduced in 1964 to guide people at each age level in their Christian life and witness. Additionally, the board prepares supplemental materials, provides field service, and assists congregations in their work of Christian nurture.

Board of Pensions

This board administers medical, disability, retirement, and survivor benefit coverage for the ministers, deaconesses, missionaries, and lay employees.

Board of Publication

The familiar imprints "Fortress Press" and "Lutheran Church Press" on books, hymnals, and parish education materials witness to the wide-ranging publishing activities of this board. The biweekly magazine *The Lutheran* is published in conjunction with the Committee on Church Papers. More than a dozen retail stores and a mammoth mail-order business provide distribution channels.

Board of Social Ministry

This board's task is to investigate the nature and implication of the church's ministry within the structures of social life as well as to guide the church in its social action whereby individual and social needs can be met as an expression of Christian responsibility for love and justice. The board engages in a variety of activities and programs: agencies and institutions serving children, aged, families; chaplaincy programs for persons in institutions; special ministries to physically and mentally handicapped; study and education in race relations, delinquency and crime, marriage and family, church-state relations, international affairs, economic matters; regular conferences for lay people in occupational groups.

Board of Theological Education

It is the specific responsibility of this board to supervise the recruitment and training of men for the Christian ministry. It seeks to accomplish this task by assisting the eleven seminaries of the church to become the best possible schools of theology.

Board of World Missions

Through this board, the Lutheran Church in America seeks to carry its share of the responsibility to proclaim the gospel to the whole world. More than 500 missionaries and 5,000 national pastors and workers minister in twelve overseas nations. In other countries, about 1,000 institutions such as elementary and secondary schools, seminaries, and hospitals have been developed by the board.

THE COMMISSIONS OF THE CHURCH

Seven commissions are established to work in areas of special concern. The size of commissions varies, and their members are appointed by the Executive Council, under whose direct supervision they work.

Commission on Church Architecture

This commission helps congregations and church-related institutions with building plans and problems. Advice is given through consultation by mail, individual conferences, and visits.

Commission on Church Papers

The families of the church have a direct contact with the Lutheran Church in America every second week through the pages of *The Lutheran*. This publication, with a biweekly circulation of well over half a million copies, is the primary responsibility of this commission.

Commission on Evangelism

Working through synodical evangelism committees, this commission seeks to guide congregations in building effective expressions and programs of concern for people who need God in their lives.

Commission on Press, Radio and T.V.

This commission is well known for the television series for children "Davey and Goliath" and the two Lutheran radio series "The Protestant Hour" and "Church World News." It also serves as press agent for the church, its officers, boards, agencies, and auxiliaries.

Commission on Stewardship

Working in close alliance with synodical stewardship committees, this commission assists congregations in the process of training their members in the practice of Christian giving. The commission is assisted by the Lutheran Laymen's Movement for Stewardship.

Commission on Worship

This commission is responsible for guiding the church in enriching worship experiences and in cultivating good liturgical practices.

Commission on Youth Activities

Working through counterpart committees in each synod and in close liaison with the Luther League, this commission is responsible for planning, structuring, and promoting programs for the youth of the church. The staff of the commission also serves as the staff of the Luther League.

The auxiliaries of the church

These auxiliaries are provided to offer opportunities for men, women, and youth in areas of witness, study, fellowship, and service.

The Lutheran Church Men

Beginning in 1967, the Lutheran Church Men exists as an auxiliary within congregations and on a synodical level. Its purpose is to mobilize and harness the manpower potential of the church to specific congregational programs such as vocational guidance, social ministry, evangelism, stewardship, and boys' work.

The Lutheran Church Women

This official auxiliary for women seeks to assist women to share fully in the life and work of the church. The organization retains an honorable legacy from the days when it was identified as a missionary society, but broadens its concept of mission to include the whole witness of church women in fuller expressions of the Christian life through a three-pronged emphasis on education, fellowship, and service.

The Luther League

Serving youth between the ages of 12 and 25, this youth organization of the church develops programs to interest youth and strengthens them for Christian service. Leadership training and guidance materials are provided. The auxiliary works through synodical units and annual conventions to accomplish its aims.

ChURCh FINANCES

The Offering

For many, the offering plate used at church services is symbolic of the church's dependence on every member to support its work. The church can only accomplish what its members enable it to do through their gifts of money, time, and talents. The offering, as its name implies, is an act of dedication in a spirit of thankfulness. We, at this moment of worship, offer ourselves and our resources for the Lord's work.

A Sense of Stewardship

Stewardship is a key word in the Christian's vocabulary. It expresses the basic attitude toward property and possessions that Christians feel indicates their gratitude toward God for his great gifts. Stewardship suggests using all that we have wisely and well. It involves conservation of our natural resources, care for our personal possessions, using our offerings to further the church's ministry to the world.

Pledging

Many congregations ask their members to pledge that they will give a certain amount of money annually to the church. Each member is free to determine according to his own conscience what this amount will be. The congregation, however, needs some estimation of what funds it can count on to develop a reasonable and practical budget for its yearly activities. Pledging is a conscious determination to support the church in its spreading of the gospel.

Special Financial Agencies of the Church

The Lutheran Laymen's Movement for Stewardship is a voluntary self-supporting men's organization designed to help each congregation build a strong stewardship program.

The Lutheran Church in America Foundation provides opportunity for members to give or will large gifts to the church for specific purposes.

Lutheran World Action and *Lutheran World Relief* are established to collect funds, clothing, food, and equipment for the needy overseas.

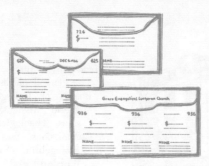

The Offering Envelope

Most congregations provide their members with weekly offering envelopes. Frequently, these envelopes have two pockets to stress the two large areas of the congregation's responsibility. Both areas are important:

Current Expenses
This part of the congregation's money is used for local expenses such as: salaries, building maintenance, utilities, supplies, equipment, music, books.

Benevolence
This part of the congregation's money goes to the work of the church on synodical, national, and international levels in areas such as missions, education, and charity.

The Calendar of Emphasis

The Calendar of Emphasis offers reminders of the total work of the church.

January: World Missions
February: American Missions
March: Evangelism
April: College Education
May: Theological Education
June: The Unity of the Church
September: Parish Education
October: Social Ministry
November: Stewardship

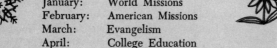

ADMINISTRATIVE OFFICES

Church House
231 Madison Avenue
New York, New York 10016

Headquarters for:
The general officers;
Boards of College Education, World Missions, Social Missions, Theological Education;
Commissions on Architecture, Evangelism, Stewardship, Worship, and Press, Radio and Television;
Lutheran Church in America Foundation.

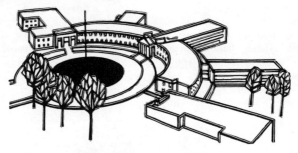

Muhlenberg Building
2900 Queen Lane
Philadelphia, Pa. 19129

Headquarters for:
Board of Parish Education;
Board of Publication;
Commission on Church Papers;
Commission on Youth Activities;
Lutheran Church Women;
Luther League;
The Lutheran magazine.

Other Locations
Board of American Missions
327 S. LaSalle Street,
Chicago, Illinois 60604

Board of Pensions
608 Second Avenue
Minneapolis, Minnesota 55402

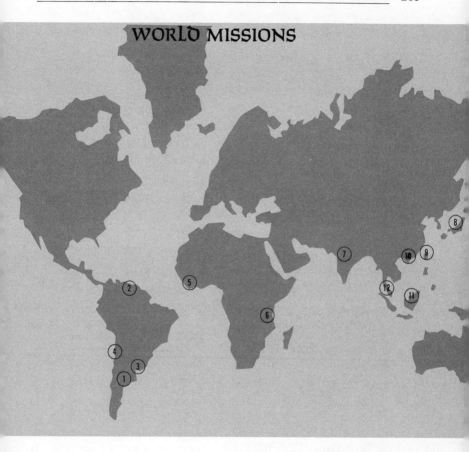

Through the Board of World Missions, the Lutheran Church in America witnesses to the Christian gospel in twelve distant countries.

1. Argentina
2. Guyana
3. Uruguay
4. Chile
5. Liberia
6. Tanzania
7. India
8. Japan
9. Taiwan (Formosa)
10. Hong Kong
11. Malaysia Sabah (North Borneo)
12. Malaysia-West (Malaya)

Colleges and Universities

Augustana College
Rock Island, Illinois
Bethany College
Lindsborg, Kansas
Carthage College
Kenosha, Wisconsin
Gettysburg College
Gettysburg, Pa.
Gustavus Adolphus College
St. Peter, Minnesota
Hartwick College
Oneonta, New York
Lenoir Rhyne College
Hickory, North Carolina
Midland Lutheran College
Fremont, Nebraska
Muhlenberg College
Allentown, Pa.
Newberry College
Newberry, South Carolina
Roanoke College
Salem, Virginia
Susquehanna University
Selinsgrove, Pa.
Thiel College
Greenville, Pa.

Upsala College
East Orange, New Jersey
Wagner College
Staten Island, New York
Waterloo Lutheran University
Waterloo, Ont., Canada
Wittenberg University
Springfield, Ohio

*Colleges with
Two-Year Program*
Grand View College
Des Moines, Iowa
Marion College
Marion, Virginia
Suomi College
Hancock, Michigan

*Cooperative,
LCA and ALC*
California Lutheran College
Thousand Oaks, California

*ALC-Owned,
LCA-Supported*
Pacific Lutheran University
Tacoma, Washington
Texas Lutheran College
Seguin, Texas
Luther College
Regina, Sask., Canada

Seminaries

Central Lutheran Theological
Seminary Fremont, Nebraska
Lutheran Theological Seminary
Philadelphia, Pa.
Lutheran Theological Seminary
Gettysburg, Pa.
Lutheran Theological
Southern Seminary
Columbia, South Carolina
Hamma School of Theology
Springfield, Ohio

Lutheran School of Theology
at Chicago
Maywood and Rock Island, Ill.
Northwestern Lutheran
Theological Seminary
Minneapolis, Minnesota
Pacific Lutheran Theological
Seminary
Berkeley, California
Lutheran Theological Seminary
Saskatoon, Sask., Canada
Waterloo Lutheran Seminary
Waterloo, Ont., Canada

COOPERATIVE AGENCIES

The National Lutheran Council
Chicago, Illinois

LCA and ALC churches cooperate through this agency to serve students, servicemen, and immigrants, and to deal with many areas of mutual social concern. In 1967 they will join with the Lutheran Church—Missouri Synod in the new *Lutheran Council in the United States of America.*

The Lutheran Council in Canada
Winnipeg, Manitoba

This cooperative agency serves Canadian Lutherans.

The Lutheran World Federation
Geneva, Switzerland

This is a worldwide federation of Lutheran churches working to coordinate Lutheran witness and service of more than 65,000,000 Lutherans. The federation provides unified procedures for international work, such as Lutheran World Action and Lutheran World Relief.

The National Council of Churches
New York, New York

Properly called the National Council of the Churches of Christ in the U.S.A., this interchurch agency is the chief organ of cooperation for most of the major denominations of this country. The council enables Protestant churches to work together creatively in many common tasks.

The World Council of Churches
Geneva, Switzerland

About 180 Protestant and Orthodox churches hold membership in the World Council, which serves as an international agency for witness and service. Since the council is composed of autonomous churches, it can neither legislate for its members nor speak for them officially. However, it can foster cooperation among Christians, develop a united witness, and constantly explore deeper relationships.

This is My Congregation

Congregation: _____ Synod: _____

    Address _____

    Phone _____

Pastor(s): _____

    Address _____

    Phone _____

Worship:

    Sunday Services _____

    Holy Communion Is Celebrated _____

    _____

Education:

    Sunday Church School _____

    Weekday Church School _____

    Vacation Church School _____

    Other Educational Opportunities _____

    _____

    _____

Parish Activities:

    Annual Congregational Meetings _____

    Election of Councilmen _____

    Auxiliaries _____

    Other Parish Activities _____

    _____